World Healing World Peace 2020

The Poets for Humanity

inner child press international

Inner Child Press International
Board of Directors

William S. Peters, Sr.
Founder ~ Publisher

hülya n. yılmaz, Ph.D.
Director of Editing Services

Gail Weston Shazor
Director of Anthologies

Kimberly Burnham, Ph.D.
Managing Director, Inner Child Magazine

Fahredin Shehu, Ph.D.
Director of Culture, International

Deborah Wilson Smart
Director of Publicity

De'Andre Hawthorne
Director, Performance Poetry

Alicja Maria Kuberska
Director of International Relations

Ashok K. Bhargava
Director

Elizabeth E. Castillo
Recording Secretary

General Information

World Healing, World Peace ~ 2020

Poets for Humanity

1st Edition: 2020

This Publishing is protected under Copyright Law as a "Collection". All rights for all submissions are retained by the individual author and or artist. No part of this Publishing may be reproduced, transferred in any manner without the prior **WRITTEN CONSENT** of the "Material Owner" or its Representative, Inner Child Press. Any such violation infringes upon the Creative and Intellectual Property of the Owner pursuant to International and Federal Copyright Law. Any queries pertaining to this "Collection" should be addressed to Publisher of Record.

Publisher Information:

Inner Child Press
intouch@innerchildpress.com
www.innerchildpress.com

This Collection is protected under U.S. and International Copyright Laws

Copyright © 2020: Inner Child Press

ISBN-13: 978-1-952081-14-9 (inner child press, ltd.)

$ 29.95

World Healing, World Peace Foundation
human beings for humanity

worldhealingworldpeacefoundation.org

Become a member of the foundation

www.worldhealingworldpeacefoundation.org

We Dedicate This Offering to...

The need within the breasts of humanity that is crying, begging, pleading and striving to be sated.

~*~

To the warriors who hold the vision without equivocation for reconciliation with a life past where suffering is no more.

~*~

To the pure of heart and the compassionate who walk amongst us and offer their light to others without reservation regardless their illusory differences.

~*~

To those who hope and dream of the 'morrow, a place of eternal serendipitous daily joys.

~*~

To the resurrection of our wonder and appreciation for all life.

~*~

To the "Believers"

www.worldhealingworldpeacepoetry.com

Table of Contents

Preface — xiii
A Few Words from the Publisher — xv
Foreword — xvii
Disclaimer — xxi

The Poetry ~ World Healing, World Peace 2020

Albert Carrasco	3
Kapardeli Eftichia	5
Alok Kumar Ray	8
Yuan Changming	10
Bharati Nayak	12
Robert Gibbons	14
Larry Blazek	16
Alicja Maria Kuberska	18
Mark Andrew Heathcote	20
Monica Maartens	23
Podakalapalli Prasad Babu	25
Bob McNeil	27
Andrew Scott	29
Hatmiati Masy'ud	32
Akhmad Cahyo Setio	34
Imer Topanica	36
Cynthia Bryant	38
Satwik Mishra	41

Table of Contents... *continued*

Gobinda Biswas	43
Anna Banasiak	45
Yvette Murrell	47
Gordana Suvajac	49
Sangepu Nageswara Rao	51
C. S. P. Shrivastava	53
Maria do Sameiro Barroso	55
Abhilash Mishra	57
Chandra Shekar Pendoti	59
Martina Reisz Newberry	61
Pushmaotee Subrun	64
Vidya Shankar	67
Shareef Abdur-Rasheed	69
Nitusmita Saikia	71
Anthony Arnold	73
Boguslawa Chwierut	75
Rohini Kumar Behera	78
Lennart Lundh	80
Kerry Brackett	82
Rickey K. Hood	84
Thaddeus Hutyra	86
Eliza Segiet	89
Danuta Blaszak	91
Anna Maria Mickiewicz	93
Christena Williams	95

Table of Contents . . . *continued*

Smruti Ranjan Mohanty	97
Snežana Šolkotović	99
B. S. Tyagi	102
Aabha Rosy Vatsa	106
Jason Constantine Ford	108
Maritza Martínez Mejía	110
Hussein Habasch	112
Fernando Martinez Alderete	115
Rubab Abdullah	117
Kay Salady	119
Tzemin Ition Tsai	122
Su Jen Lin	124
Soma Bhowmik	126
Ushie James Obule	128
Christine Von Lossberg	130
Egbung Elizabeth Omaku	132
Priya Unnikrishnan	136
Tanja Ajtic	138
Otteri Selvakumar	140
Orbindu Ganga	142
Norbert Góra	145
Pankhuri Sinha	147
Deema Mahmood	149
Elena Liliana Popescu	151

Table of Contents . . . *continued*

Krishna Prasai	158
Louise Hudon	161
Naida Mujkić	164
Tarana Turan Rahimli	166
Francisca Ricinski	169
Abdel-Wahed Souayah	171
Ali Abukhattab	173
Parneet Jaggi	175
Kimberly Burnham	177
Pavol Janik	180
Neetu Vaid Sharma	182
Monalisa Dash Dwibedy	184
Ashok Bhargava	186
Sandra Mooney-Ellerbeck	188
Nassira Nezzar	190
Anwar Ghani	193
Othmen Mahdi	195
Sylwia K. Malinowska	198
Sudarsan Sahu	200
Kamar Sultana Sheik	202
Elizabeth Esguerra Castillo	204
Santosh Kumar Biswa	206
hülya n. yılmaz	208
Teresa E. Gallion	211

Table of Contents . . . *continued*

Alicia Minjarez Ramirez	213
Monsif Beroual	216
Eden Soriano Trinidad Blooms	218
Zaldy Carreon De Leon, Jr.	221
Romeo R. Agustin, Jr.	226
Metin Cengiz	228
Ibrahim Honjo	230
Shiv Raj Pradhan	233
Hema Ravi	235
Nicholas Shifrar	237
Mamu Roshid	241
Houda Elfchtali	243
Brian Callahan	246
Caroline 'Ceri Naz' Nazareno-Gabis	249
Muhammad Azram	251
Ivan Gaćina	254
Noreen Ann Snyder	256
Hamid Larbi	258
Ashu Arora	260
Lily Swarn	262
Fahredin Shehu	264
Maria Fernanda vila Migliaro	266
Mounira Ahmed	268
Azza Issa	270

Table of Contents... *continued*

Mohamed Abdel Aziz Shmeis	272
Zainab Muhammad Aboud	274
Salah Zangana	276
Habiba Gharib	278
Achwak Chaichi	280
Sumaya Al-Hamayda	282
Abdel Fattah Shehata	284
Emiliano Pintos	286
Angelica Cristina Garcia	288
David Haotian Dai	290
Nataša Sardžoska	292
Faleeha Hassan	295
William S. Peters, Sr.	297
Previous issues of World Healing, World Peace	301

Preface

The inspiration for a global anthology of this content lies in the heart-driven observations of the contributors. World's preventable ills are evident. A united look at the pain and sufferings of the innocent against the backlash of available solutions blocked by those in power was a sufficient reason for us to feel motivated to collectively appeal to our readership. We knew that we had to stand up and be counted when our joint conviction was concerned: to help combat at least some of the tribulations that are inflicted upon the powerless by countless men / women, driven by the greed for money and hatred toward everyone who is different.

As for the genre of focus, poetry has been known for ages to enable that which seems impossible for those trapped in silence for one reason or another: a voice. The plea voiced in this publication for you, dear reader, is simple: world peace. In order to achieve peace on a global scale, however, the process of healing must materialize across the world. Addressing the ills is a start, in addition to being a vital step. Hence, some poems in this volume bring such efforts to your attention. Others only speak of the post-healing state of an individual or a group of people. Unanimously, though, each poet's work in this volume aims to come to terms with the dilemmas and struggles that affect humanity at large. It is that noble intent which brought a large number of writers together for and through this poetry compilation.

The world regions from and the languages with which an excess of 120 poets arrived at this destination constitute a vast number. Their insights into and contemplations on the critical importance of world healing, world peace entered this publication – either in translations or in the contributors' original tongues –from Greece, India, China, Poland, Slovakia, South Africa, Indonesia, Kosova, Pakistan, former Yugoslavia, Portugal, the Republic of Mauritius, Jamaica, Australia, Kurdistan, Mexico, Bangladesh, Taiwan,

Nigeria, Canada, Egypt, Romania, Nepal, Bosnia, Azerbaijan, Tunisia, Palestine, Algeria, Iraq, the Philippines, the Kingdom of Bhutan, Turkey, Morocco, Croatia, Algiers, Uruguay, Syria, Jordan, Chile, Peru, the U.K. and the U.S.A.

The rigid linguistic demands native speakers of English make on non-natives can be utterly restrictive to literary voices across the world that have much to add to our minds' expansion, but to our overall enrichment as individuals as well. A considerable number of the contributors speak several languages, on which we have neither jurisdiction nor first-hand knowledge. Yet, we, in the English-speaking regions of the globe, have the tendency to dictate the non-native speakers and writers of our target language how to speak and write. Furthermore, the pressure we place on them reaches a point of forcing them to think how we do. Instead of honoring the wealth of insights they offer us, either in translation or through their unique ways of expression using English, we are quick to judge the surface differences. Poetic creativity, however, does not work thus.

If you are an English-only speaker, our collection of poems will demand from you to expand your comfort zone. For, none of the authorial messages has been edited for content. Our decision was, as it always is with our international anthologies, to honor and preserve the authentic voices of the contributing poets. Therefore, only minor changes were made in specific terms of mechanical rules, as widely expected in the U.S.A. So, we invite you to take delight in the diverse formulations of the poetic art and the multiple voices of genuine concern for an all-inclusive humanity, while you take note of the unique beauty in the distinctive verse-paintings that enabled this anthology. You will not be disappointed.

hülya n. yılmaz

Ph.D., Liberal Arts Emerita
The Pennsylvania State University

a few words from the Publisher

I am not quite sure if the strife within our world has escalated any more in recent times since our last edition in 2018, but most certainly, thanks to the internet, our awareness of the global situation has increased.

When I think of the aspect of accomplishing World Healing, World Peace, I am left with no other choice but to be a believer . . . yes, "I Am a Believer"!

With that being said, ergo our efforts as conscious human beings, we offer our words to that end . . . World Healing, World Peace.

As we look across the globe, our world, there is much suffering that manifests itself in war, hunger, disease, homelessness, greed, oppression, racism, bias, abuse and molestation, etc. Conversely, I see much light as well. It is evidenced right here in our 6th volume of *World Healing, World Peace*. Here, you can read the voices of the many contributors who offer their perspectives in a poetic form. When I consider the possibilities our life experience offers, it is quite poetic in nature. Beyond the ugliness we humans are capable of, there is a prevailing beauty that is begging to be indulged by the masses. This is the light I speak of that we all possess within. I believe in this light. I believe in you, the greater you! There once was a prophet who said, "greater is that which is within you than that which is within the world". I am a believer . . . how about you?

So, take a moment and read the offered poetic words here and consider the perspectives of other human beings just like yourself. Consider their cries for peace and reconciliation with our humanity. Hear their anger and confusion, their chaotic cries for change. Listen to your own heart begging for that certainty of peace and healing on an existential basis.

Bless Up

'Just Bill'
William S. Peters, Sr.

Foreword

In the world, there are many ways to say "Peace": "Paz", "Paix", "Damai", "Heping", "Shānti", "Shalom" "Salaam", "Vrede", "Mwarre" . . . Each word is made of sounds, musical tones holding a sphere of meanings, connecting one to another. Each sound carries a feeling from the heart of the speaker. Words land in unique and beautiful ways on the listener's ear. In the speaker's throat, the meaning of the words are not all the same, just as we, the seven billion of us that share this planet with the plants, animals and other living creatures are exceptional. If we come together, share and speak words of peace and healing, we may all thrive and live good lives.

W—We, like the Ancient Mayans of Mexico's Yucatan peninsula, can find peace and more in "Ciciol" which means peace, joy, pleasure, and happiness in this land near the warm ocean. As you read and live, listen for "Cici" meaning pleasant, agreeable, or originally what is pleasant to taste. What do peace and healing taste like?

O—Order and clarity can bring peace and healing. Abaknon speakers find peace in order and clarity. "Malînaw" means peaceful, calm, clear, legible, to clear up, make clear, clarify, settle and pacify on the Sama-Bajaw Capul Island of the Philippines.

R—Recall a journey and the words that kept you safe. "Amniat" in Pashto, a language of Afghanistan and Iran means peace but also safety and safe to pass. Imagine calling to another on a journey around the world, "Amniat!"

L—Let those in need of healing find comfort in these words. In Indonesian Kaili Ledo, "Nompakabelo" means to make peace but also to cure or to fix. World healing is baked into the world peace with "Nompakabelo!"

D—"Dagom" is one word in Takia, an Oceanic language of Papua New Guinea. We find peace and tameness together here. May we each discover peace and tameness in the world as we ponder "Dagom!"

H—Healing words can bring "Sges" peace or wellbeing in the language of the Spokane-Kalispel-Flathead tribes in Washington and Idaho in the United States. Speak wellbeing into this day, "Sges!"

E—Ease into the words, find the places where there is comfort for you. "llonydd" means peace, still, stationary, and calm in Welsh spoken in the United Kingdom. Find and share a magical place of "llonydd!"

A—Aymara, a language spoken in Peru and Bolivia, emboldens the word "Qasiki" with 'peaceful', 'tranquil' and 'free'. Visualize a mountain peak high above the clouds as light and darkness play together near the sun and there is peace and freedom manifest in a word, "Qasiki!"

L—Let peace lift you. "Marrparaŋ" is peace, security, brave, and fearless in Dhaŋu, spoken on Elcho Island and Yirrkala in Australia. Be brave with "Marrparaŋ!"

I—In IsiZulu of South Africa, "Ukuba nokuthula" is peace of mind, while "Nokuthula" is mother of peace, and "Izingane zokuthula" means children of peace. Envision a world where mothers, children and all enjoy "" nokuthula!"

N—In Éwé, a Niger-Congo language of West Africa, peace is there in coolness. "Ŋutifafa" means peace as skin become cold or cool. "Fáfá" is peace. "Fá" means to become cold or cool, associated with good feelings in "Fáfá!"

G—Go forth, read, listen, speak "Konyo" means peaceful and quiet in the Romany of the Travelers in Europe and South America. May we all be speakers of peace and listeners of safety, tameness, bravery, satisfaction, warmth and coolness. See all the good in the world and what each one of us can share with our time, resources, healing skills but above all love and "Konyo!"

Kimberly Burnham

Spokane, Washington

Disclaimer

In our attempts to maintain the integrity of the voices of the 'Poets for Humanity', we have elected to do minimal surface editing. We felt that preserving the original entries was critically important for you, the reader, to enjoy each poet's authenticity.

You may encounter a few challenges in achieving total clarity of the messages shared through poetry, but I indulge you to let go of your critical thinking and embrace the spirit through words offered, pertaining this meaningful theme of World Healing, World Peace 2020.

From the desk of hülya n. yılmaz, Ph.D.
Director of Editing

Inner Child Press International

'building bridges of cultural understanding'

The Poetry for World Healing World Peace 2020

World Healing ~ World Peace 2020

World Healing ~ World Peace 2020

Albert 'Infinite the Poet' Carrasco is from the Bronx, New York. He is a published urban poet. 'Infinite' mentally rewinds time in order to narrate his past. He uses his experiences of poverty, drugs, jail and murder as educational opportunities for others. He feels that writing to save lives is his purpose.

Reach Out

We have to do better. Reach out to people you grew up with because life is short, people are fighting demons of all sorts, depression, addiction, loneliness, unhealthy thoughts, etcetera, etcetera. We can't assume people are doing okay because during the time of assumption people are slipping away. Some individuals reach out, others stray. Some pop up, text or call, others feel like they're stuck between four closing walls. Mask are being worn. Silent suffering is common, I can't let the world see my pain . . . I can't let my problems become someone else's problem . . . no one cares . . . people are happy that I'm in this position . . . are thoughts while they battle their demon. Look at him, he's doing good. Look at her, she's doing well. Look at all of them, they're all fine. When is it going to be my time? Everything you see isn't always what it is, nowadays almost everything is sensationalized, especially social media with its visual lies. Made up lifestyles go viral while others feel like they're not keeping up with the status quo so the earth's rotation sends them into a downward spiral.

We all go through trial and tribulations. Speak about it. Voicing concerns and receiving advice can change situations.

World Healing ~ World Peace 2020

Kapardeli Eftichia has a doctorate from the Arts and Culture World Academy. She lives in Patras where she writes poetry (including haiku), short prose and essays. She studied journalism in AKEM. She has many awards from national competitions, and her work has appeared in many national and international anthologies. She has a program at the University of Cyprus on Greek culture. [. . .]

eftichiakapa.blogspot.gr/2013/08/blog-post_4143.html

World Healing ~ World Peace 2020

Χρυσα Ονειρα

Στο χρόνο ασυλλόγιστα
τους εαυτούς μας ξοδέψαμε

με τις λευκές νιφάδες
του χιονιού
μοναχικά σμιλέψαμε
Μα την αγάπη φυλαχτό
κρατήσαμε

στα όνειρα των κοριτσιών
στις φτωχογειτονιές
του κόσμου

στο κλάμα ενός πεινασμένου
παιδιού
στην αγωνία ,στον φόβο,
στην
απόγνωση, στην
προσμονή στην
οδύνη μιας λαβωμένης
καρδιάς
που δίψασε για αγάπη,
προσκυνητές και βοηθοί
μείναμε

Τις δύσκολες ώρες της νύχτας
αντέξαμε
προσμένοντας τον Ήλιο
τις χούφτες μας με
φως να γεμίσουμε
τα μυστικά περάσματα
να φωτίσουμε
με τα φωτεινά του βέλη
τις ανθρώπινες καρδιές
να λαβώσουμε
χρυσά όνειρα
να χαρίσουμε

World Healing ~ World Peace 2020

Golden Dreams

In time immoral
we spent ourselves

with white flakes
of snow
we lonely chiseled
But the love
talisman
we kept it

in the dreams of girls
in the slums
of the world
in the cry of a hungry
child
in anxiety, in fear,
in despair, in
expectation at
the suffering of a loser
heart

thirst for love,
pilgrims and assistants
we stayed

The tough hours of the night
we endured
expecting the Sun
our handfuls with
light to fill
the secret passages

to shine
with its bright arrows
the human hearts
to hurt
Golden Dreams
to give away

Dr. Alok Kumar Ray is a bilingual poet (both Odia and English) whose poems have been featured in a number of anthologies and journals of national and international repute. He has attended many national and international poetry gatherings. Currently, he resides in the JAJPUR district headquarters in Odisha, India.

Peace

"Do you believe in peace?"
Said the protagonist who by default
Didn't see in anybody any fault
Sunshine while touching everybody
Differentiates none, "Does it favour anybody?"
The dove of peace is capacitated to fly everywhere
Inherited it the stamina to propagate love and fraternity there
Flapping of its wings is very phenomenal
I was a little bit skeptical
My thoughts went up vertically
No, no . . . said someone inside me! Made it I horizontal steadily
Healing a wound needs compassion
Doctor's prescription is not at all an aberration
Shallowing medicines . . . well is what relieves us from contradictions
Relied heavily the ardent progeny of peace on these narrations
I was recovering from my long hibernation
Decided without any second thought to go up from pretention
Said I with utmost humble and submission
Shedding of blood is almost de facto which we really resort to
Stunning is giving blood which we are not accustomed to
World peace is not only an idea to deify
A pious sermon that even an atheist can't nullify
It's translation, execution in real parlance
Let it become the panacea that heals all ills at a glance

World Healing ~ World Peace 2020

Yuan Changming published monographs on translation before leaving China with a Canadian Ph.D. in English. Changming currently edits *Poetry Pacific* with Allen Yuan in Vancouver. Credits include ten Pushcart nominations and publications in *Best of the Best Canadian Poetry* (2008-17) & *BestNewPoemsOnline,* which is among the 1,569 other literary outlets across 42 countries.

Making Light of the Darkness

In a world perpetually half in darkness
Your body may be soaked deep
In a wet nightmare, rotting

But your heart can roam
Like a synchronous satellite
In the outer space, leaving
The long night far behind

As long as your heart flies fast
& high enough, you will live
Forever in light

World Healing ~ World Peace 2020

Bharati Nayak is a bilingual poet, critique and translator from Bhubaneswar, India. Her poems have been published in many reputed magazines and journals such as *The Tranquil Muse, Rock Pebbles, Orissa Review, Creation and Criticism, Circular Whispers, Nova Literature-Poesis, Poetry Against Terror, 56 Female Voices of Poetry, The Four Seasons Poetry Concerto*. [. . .]

Mourning the Death of Innocent Flowers

Take not the name of any religion
As God would never pardon
Spilling of innocent blood
You are game to treacherous designs of wicked minds
Who are bent upon destroying human kind
They have their own selfish end
And use you as puppets
When you should have played with ball
They put bombs in your hands
When you should have played violin
They gave the gun to fire.

See how flowers have died
In your heart and in your garden
The demon darkens
The sky choking light to death
Music falls silent
Every rhythm joyful dies
Devil dances in the heart of those
Who chose
Hell over heaven
I pray for the innocent flowers
That have died in you and in the garden

Robert Gibbons, a native Floridian, came to New York City in 2007 in search of his muse, Langston Hughes, and found a vibrant contemporary poetry community at the Cornelia Street Cafe, the Green Pavilion, Nomad's Choir, Brownstone Poets, Hydrogen Juke Box, Saturn Series, and Phoenix among other venues. His first book, *Close to the Tree*, was published by the New York-based Three Rooms Press in 2012. [. . .]

A Metaphor for a Clipper

1. a person or thing that clips or cuts.
2. Often, clippers. (*often used with a plural verb*) a cutting tool, especially shears: *hedge clippers.*
3. Usually, clippers. (*usually used with a plural verb*) a mechanical or electric tool for cutting hair, fingernails, or the like: *He told the barber, "No clippers on the sides, please."*
4. *Nautical.* Also called clipper ship. a sailing ship built and rigged for speed, especially a type of three-masted ship with a fast hull form and a lofty rig, built in the U.S. from c1845, and in Great Britain from a later date, until c1870, and used in trades in which speed was more important than cargo capacity.
5. *Electronics.* A device that gives output only for an input above or below a certain critical value.

It is ashamed I have to layer you metaphor;
to prove that I am just as authentic as anyone;
it is ashamed I have to repeatedly prove
that every definition applies; to rise
from the middle of the passage; the last vestiges
of antebellum; hate to be histrionic with my remonstrance;
to use fifty cents words; but this, a code; as black and as
fugitive as this outmoded intent; every definition applies
to you; if this were a list poem; I could use invective or
pejorative or expletive; or just crow; just a cutting tool;
just a mower, a coward; a bastard; a fowl; a goose; a senseless

beast; he told the barber, no clippers on the side; no black, no
Jews, no Catholics; no Baptists; no Mormons; no mourners
no polygamist; no definition for you; lost in the translation; I am
done with metaphor, so let's go folklore; William Dean Howells;
and Joel Chandler Harris; a parrot that mimics his master; the titanic
of disaster; imagine a keel of a ship; imagine a Freudian slip and then
there is you; the lonely you; the forgery of ink; that sinks in subtext;
the footnote; the hoax; and then there is just one definition left; this
take all the breath; will call it electronic; first there is sound; then
phonics; then words; then sentence; then repentance; then
the judgment. Oh, I rather you plural, it keeps it more truthful.

World Healing ~ World Peace 2020

Larry Blazek was born in Northern Indiana, but moved to the southern part because the climate there is more suited to cycling and the land is cheap. He has been publishing the magazine-format collage, "Opossum Holler Tarot" since 1983 and could use some submissions. He has been published in the "The Bat Shat", "Vox Poetica", "Leveler Poetry", "Five Fishes", "Front", and "Mountain Focus Art", among many other poetic platforms.

The White Parade

peace rests uneasily
upon the war-torn people
huddling fearfully
in the ruins of their city
no one cheers the parade
of the new leaders
who still address the people
at gun point
a war-torn people
used to shooting
anyone in uniform
no one is shot this day
soldiers clean debris
from the street
one by one people
emerge from the ruins
to help them live in peace

Alicja Maria Kuberska is an awarded Polish poetess, novelist, journalist, editor. She edited many volumes in both, Polish and English. Her poems have been published in numerous anthologies and magazines in Poland, the Czech Republic, Slovakia, the UK, Belgium, Bulgaria, Hungary, Albania, Spain, Italy, Turkey, Argentina, Chile, Peru, Mexico, Israel, the USA, Canada, India, Uzbekistan, Saudi Arabia, South Korea, Taiwan, China, South Africa, Zambia and Australia. [. . .]

War in the Middle East

Memories like grains of sand,
during a storm in the desert,
swirl violently in the mind.
They hit hard, hurt badly.

Eye wanders around a desolate city
I remember, a school was there
and next to it a library and a flower shop.
Huge cavities in the ground gape instead
surrounded by charred tree stumps.

Silence spills in a wide stream
over empty streets and ashes,
settling like dust on broken glass.
Birds flew away, the absent inhabitants fell silent.
Wind wails among the ruins and then,
as echo, the whistle of falling bombs returns.

In a surviving building without a wall,
as if on a great theatrical stage of life,
an old man sits alone, reading a book.
Hunger and fear drove neighbors away
He did not run, and became a guardian of hope

Poor people suffer and die.
Politicians speak beautifully of peace,
democracy, and human rights.
Greedy businessmen count profits
from the trade of weapons.

Vampires hover over the oil fields
swabbing the last drops of black blood
from the tormented desert land.

Mark Andrew Heathcote is from Manchester, UK. He is the author of two poetry books, *In Perpetuity* and *Back on Earth*, published by a CTU publishing group, Creative Talents Unleashed. He began writing poetry during his early schooling. He is a support worker in adult learning difficulties. The author enjoys spending his leisure time off work reading and writing and spending time gardening.

https://www.ctupublishinggroup.com/mark-andrew-heathcote.html

World Healing ~ World Peace 2020

Mother Teresa, the Mission of Charity

She joined the Sisters of Loreto age 18 years
Had a 40yr faith crisis, yet has been canonized.
Taking her vows as a nun in 1931 her life blurs.
"Peace of heart", she never developed one
She'd a calling to enter the slums she-agonized
Distressed by what she saw and thereupon,

She gave up all gave up searching for peace
To this end, she gave her heart to Jesus
Her call, that wasn't seen the lease bit caprice?
She aided the dying the poor in Calcutta.
She helped the sick to battle diseases
She doesn't feign to like the slums or those gutters.

But she wanted to help eradicate poverty,
Eliminate hunger and help heal the sick.
While all the time she struggled and conversely
Prayed for guidance to strengthen her faith,
Holding hands with the insane the lunatic
She made a difference in her humble ways,

She jarred a door wide, showed a needless path
If there were more like her willing to help?
And dedicate help to healing the psychopath,
Help sucker the emaciated heart of humanity
War, could be eradicated, hunger expelled
And peace, faith could reign enigmatically.

On even her Mother Teresa's wrinkled face
But she felt deeply, alone quite abandoned
This void of emptiness at times took its place
She lived in a state of spiritual pain,
But her resolve to help never dampened
From 12yrs of age—knew her path, been preordain.

World Healing ~ World Peace 2020

She opened; open a hospice for the poor
A home for, orphans and homeless youths
Herself, 15yrs-living in a hovel furthermore
Opened another for the sufferers of leprosy
Yes, I guess she was saintly, you want proofs?
Leave your riches; homes spread her kind of equity.

World Healing ~ World Peace 2020

Monica Maartens prefers to be addressed by "Zararia Yul", her penname, meaning "brightness of dawn river beyond the horizon". She has chosen this name after her training in the university of life, darkness and during severe tribulations, having to conquer many battles of all kinds . . . now, sharing her knowledge with the world through poetry.

Stop for a Moment

Stop for a moment and look around,
earth is reeling under humanities noise,
rebellion and destruction are causing havoc,
disturbing the tranquility of earthly rhythm.

Stop for a moment and take careful note,
earth is rising to its own defense,
echoing all the disturbances and rebellion,
roaring its displeasure of humanity.

Stop for a moment and think what we can do,
how we can bring peace into hearts untrue,
cast out hatred in exchange for love,
heal the brokenness and make all whole.

Stop for a moment and bow in prayer,
give God space to bring repair,
cast away the wicked darkness,
touch all humanity with love divine,
wipe all tears and remove all fears,
bring back all the joyful laughter,
heal the world with glorious peace,
break all chains and give captives release.

World Healing ~ World Peace 2020

P.S.V. Prasad Babu is working as a School Assistant (Eng.) at the Govt. High School in Medarabasti, Kothagudem, Bhadradri – Kothagudem Dist, Telangana State. He has three master degrees from Kakatiya University, Warangal in English, Economics and Education. He has been qualified for APSET in the subject of Economics in 2014. He has ten years of teaching experience in English at the high school level. [. . .]

Our Teachers

We ever interest go to school
When the weather is too cool
By luck we have good teachers
They thought us as peace preachers

They trained us as great orators
To make as future peace protectors
And if we won't made plans for rains
We have to face number of future pains

They said don't be moody
Work harder on study
And sweet and fabulous honey
Is valuable than manmade money

They thought harmfulness of swords
And importance of peace words
To make this world as so sweet
With our love and peace tweet.

World Healing ~ World Peace 2020

Bob McNeil is the author of *Verses of Realness*. Hal Sirowitz, Queens Poet Laureate, described the book as "A fantastic trip through the mind of a poet who doesn't flinch at the truth." Bob was published in *The Shout It Out Anthology*, *Brine Rights: Stanzas and Clauses for the Causes (Volume 1)*, *San Francisco Peace and Hope*, and *The Self-Portrait Poetry Collection*, etc. [. . .]

http://www.undergroundbooks.org/bob-mcneil.html

Download an Upward View

Press Esc
When your Thoughtfulness Program
Won't open or
Press Control, Alt, and Delete
If still stuck
In a rancor-mannered mode.
Anytime intolerance installs
Itself with a spam virus'
Tenaciousness,
Log out of Hate
And reboot your
Compassion.
Wait, then
Log into something humane,
Use your Solicitude App
So it won't happen again.

Andrew Scott is a native of Fredericton, NB. During his time as an active poet, Andrew Scott has taken the time to speak in front of classrooms, judge poetry competitions as well as being published worldwide in such publications as The Art of Being Human, Battered Shadows and The Broken Ones. His books, *Snake with A Flower, The Phoenix Has Risen, The Path, The Storm Is Coming* and *Through My Eyes* are available now. *Searching* is the title of his fifth poetry collection. [. . .]

http://andrewmscott.com

World Healing ~ World Peace 2020

Let Us All Rise

In a state of holy prayer
a church mass exploded with fire.
A Suicide bomber takes away their night.
Shattered remains all taken
from the sanctuary in Alexandria,
heard all across the Egyptian sky.

The terrorist created a river of blood
that they screamed was owed and deserved.
Time has taken away too many
by the masked bullies on this night.
Let us all rise and take it all back
and make it all ours and peaceful again.

In a Turkish cafe, visitors enjoying a day break
not knowing that two amongst them
had plans with a gun and their lives.
People from all over the world
never to see families or home again
due to the gun-firing cowards.

The assault rifles two men
want to lay claim to the innocent
for reasons only they truly know.
Let us rise against the violence
in the center of our lives
where bravery begins with living.

Chinese kindergarten, lined with our future,
blasted into the sky.
No one knew if it was an accident
or triggered by the hand of hate.

World Healing ~ World Peace 2020

The world around us is blowing up
into the darkness of the night.
The monsters are taking it bit by bit
without a true blown fight.

It is time we marched
with all of our unified spirit
where kindness brings comfort.
It is time we took it all back
with screams of passion
and no more fear, let us all rise.

Hatmiati Masy'ud was born in South Kalimantan, Indonesia, where her literary works in the form of short stories and poems have been published, among others in *Sun Picking Women* (Anthology Together, 2016), *Pilanggur* (a Banjar language anthology, 2017, for which she has received the Literature Rancage 2018 award), and *Selendang Mayang* (Anthology Together, 2017).

hatmiati.masyud@gmail.com

World Healing ~ World Peace 2020

Our Earth

Earth is ours
You're in the East and I'm in the West
You're in the South and I'm in the North
You're upstream and I'm downstream
You're in the ocean and I'm on land
we are on the same earth

Earth is our home
inheritance of grandparents
we guard, we maintain
disputes are of no use
the cry of war and hatred
because it only makes sorrow

Our palace is earth
where we were born and returned
place of knitting hope
embroidering dreams
share happiness
for the same ideals and love

Akhmad Cahyo Setio is a literary activist from Banjarmasin Indonesia. He has participated in various regional and international literary activities. His poems were included in numerous such poetry anthologies, including *Amaravati Poem Prism* (2018 India), *the best choice poem in the international poetry anthology, "Just Love Me"* (Nepal, India 2019), at the international Malays Festival (Singapore 2018). [. . .]

Akgmadcahyosetio@gmail.com

Like a Drop of Burned Water

I wanna see the Sun tomorrow
I wanna feel the warm embrace

I'm like a drop of water
Suck away burned hot fire
I was like a small tree, dry without leaves

I miss my Mom
I miss my Daddy
I miss all my brothers

Then when I miss my Mom, I hug dust on the Earth
Then when I miss my father, I look at the mountain soaring
If I miss my brothers
Their little rocks like them

I miss all of them
Don't take them all from me
I wanna live quietly, peacefully and happily as they say

But the reality is, I am alone
Nobody
Live in the cruelty of the world

Imer Topanica, born in 1983, is a poet and a writer from Kosova. He is the author of two books: *UDHËTARËT* (Princi, Tirana 2013); *TUFË DRITE* (Rrokullia, Pristina 2014). His miscellaneous poems and short stories were published by Jeta e Re, Akademia, Verbi, Ilz, and more.

Come, I Am Calling Thee Affectionately

Come to this fire and take the warmth
Take it to kindle your path.
Mock me not, for I keep whirling and
dancing around this light.

What a joy it brings, only my soul knows
What a never-ending dance, join me!
The more the dancers, the blither the soul

Come, the pupil can't see this light
Come, only the bliss of the soul knows this warmth
Come, vanish not into the darkness, o' brother of mine
For the tree is withering away in solitude and lovelessness

Come, because upon hatred sprout just plants of hate
And the fruits they ripe, evoke nothing but the curse
Come to my dancing near this eternal fire
Until before death tear us apart, we turned not this small world into hell

Translated by Visar Zeka

World Healing ~ World Peace 2020

Cynthia Bryant has been writing, publishing and reading her poetry for 20+years. She served as Poet Laureate for Pleasanton, Ca 2005-2007 & 2011-2013. The author now lives in Monterey, Ca where she lives with her spouse, Allen and fur-babies Oscar Wilde and Gracie Mae. Cynthia hosts the monthly venue, Last Sundays' Fishbowl Poetry.

cynthialanebryant.com

White Supremacy

Am I really superior,
how can that be?
Thin-skinned milky white
created in absence of love
sold on the black market
I crawled on bloodied knees
through emotional obscurity
to now

As I look about I see every hue
of upright human doings
Flesh tones run the gamut
of albino white to darkest night
happily house souls
the family of human kind
Even color of eyes
give little hint
of what character of soul
peers through

Each have sulked between poverty
to increments of gilded wealth
Kneeled down to many or no god
Experienced joy and loss

Beside the necessary differences
of male to female anatomy
and amorphous others
spectrum of all remains the same

Have the same vicious fluids
that maintain life on the inside
loosen each moment when interrupted
erupted to air, flowing on the ground
Circle the drain

World Healing ~ World Peace 2020

Our emotions are all that separate souls
allow self-loathing
hatred of others to divide us
We cannot detect from sight
that which makes that atom split
makes us destructive to one another

Superiority does not exist
In a world where all
were created from stardust
misfit genes that only enhance
imperfections

Hailing from India, Satwik Mishra graduated in B. Tech from the VIT University in 2014. Later on, he proceeded with his studies in DEBM, PGDRD, PGDFGR and PGDTDM. Meanwhile, he has also completed the SBI Youth for India Fellowship and the SPARC Fellowship, for which he worked on multiple projects in the area of development, i.e. establishing a science lab in the rural schools of Odisha and getting solar LED street lights installed in all Gram Panchayats. [. . .]

The Global Citizen

I don't have any caste,
I don't belong to any religion,
Environment is my biggest asset,
Inner-Peace is my ultimate aim.
Love is the only language I speak,
Co-existence is the ideology I believe in,
Earth is the society I live in.

You must be worrying about my citizenship now.
Yeah . . . I am the Global Citizen

World Healing ~ World Peace 2020

The English poems of Gobinda Biswas have been published in the print anthology, *Let There be Peace* by Dr. Deen Dayal (U.P., India, June 02, 2018); the online magazine, *Different Truths* by Arindam Roy (Uttar Pradesh, India, September 10, 2018); the print anthology, *Tranquil Muse* by Gopichand P. and Nagasuseela P. (Guntur, Andhra Pradesh, India, September 21, 2018); *The Petals of Peace*. [. . .]

The Same Is Human Blood

You may be a Hindu, Muslim or Christian
Or a Buddhist, Zoroastrian, Pagan or Jew,
You are orthodox in your religion
You propagate own supremacy anyhow.

You always forget the fundamental truth
That Nature created man through evolution,
Not the so-called God created man
Whereas man created God and religion.

You are busy with your false religion
Which always despises the true humanism,
If they are not the followers of your religion
They are Devil, you forget the philanthropism.

So, gradually you get severely violent
You kill them and destroy their holy shrines,
You molest their women, children are victimized
But you fall ill and need blood to save life hence.

You cry aloud, 'Save me, save me please'
Now I need human blood but no religion,
You are transmitted the blood of an unbeliever
Like Christ you resurrect with a bright opinion.

Anna Banasiak is a poet and an occupational therapist. Her poems have been published in New York, London, Surrey, Australia, Canada, India, Africa, Japan, China, Cuba, and Israel. She belongs to Kamena, the Micropoetry Society, and Japan Poets Association. She is the winner of the first prize recipient in Berlin; the winner of the UNESCO medal in London; the winner of a poetry competition in Bratislava; the winner at Poems and Quotes, Writers Cafe, poem of the day at poemhunter, poem of the month at poetbay. [. . .]

World Healing ~ World Peace 2020

The Music of Peace

the world is whirling too fast
people change masks in naive masquerade
nations conquer nations under the walls of prejudice
under the dark blue sky free from wars and screams
I hear the music of Peace
it's like the rustle of wings
fragile but unforgettable
people can also hear this beautiful music
when they look at each other like brothers
who can heal the world with one good word
with one look and deed
and then the angelic music of peace
can lift the world to harmony and happiness

World Healing ~ World Peace 2020

Yvette Murrell is a Power Voice & Choice Coach, who has a multifaceted background in business, education, nonprofits and the creative arts. She believes in big belly laughter and dreams of a life sweet beyond her imagination. She plays with these identities: a twin, a mother, a facilitator, an artist, an alchemist, and a writer.

http://yvettemurrell.com/

Bridges

Joy can only go so far when you won't hold pain.
Life can only go so far when you won't hold death.
Shared humanity is about holding both with love and integrity.
This is a challenging place to stand and a powerful place to be.

Recognize how the past is useful to bring love to the present.
Recognize how dreaming is useful to generate the future.
Recognize how understanding lives in relevant metaphors.
Recognize the work generated by painful experiences.
Recognize the opportunity to love, accept, forgive and cherish all.
Recognize the invitation to be authentic, feel and be with what is.
Recognize the choice to be present and hold meaningful boundaries.
Recognize when you are free, someone is holding the container in which you are twirling.
Recognize where you are listening from.
Recognize where you are observing from.
Recognize where you are now.
If you have it, build the bridge to connect with others. If not, welcome them on the journey.
If they choose not to build the bridge to the part of themselves that is reflected in you, then remember when you were there and give them permission not to connect. Give them permission to be in separation and bless them with love for their journey. Then weep for the pain of separation and let the tears become rivers, let rivers become oceans and let mother earth spew her lava blood into the ocean, building new island bridges of her own.

World Healing ~ World Peace 2020

The author of ten books of poetry, Gordana Suvajac, was born in 1962 in Srbac, a small city of former Yugoslavia. She studied at a university in Novi Sad. Later on, she moved to Belgrade to work, and started a family there. Just before the onset of war in the region, she migrated to Australia where she lives today. [. . .]

World Healing ~ World Peace 2020

Live in Peace

Beautiful world turned to hell.
Paradise that had gone and fell.
Hear the bells.
Escape the shell, the one confining truth.

Humanity shall reintroduce.
It's not too late,
to save the Earth from its fatal fate.

Shine bright, among the fading lights.
Share love with all of one's might.
We must heal from pain, and face the fright.
Live in peace and raise the light.

World Healing ~ World Peace 2020

Sangepu Nageswara Rao is working as a junior lecturer of English in the Government Junior College of Burgampahad, which belongs to the Badradri Kothagudem Dist. 9849215838. He wrote three poems and one fantasy novel. He is also a social activist.

World Healing ~ World Peace 2020

Peace Is in Our Hearts

A dark and light in our world
keep with care with a hand
a young and old faces on fight
for a goal is our world becomes peace.

A stranger and a country man together
an enemy and enemy are now friends
but all the people helping each other
for getting back with peace.

A soulmate comes from our soul
our heart understanding another
all the people feeding their elders
with the same customs and bowls.

Peace is our inner voice
remove from our wars
hands together between our nations
to get peace with your family members.

Make you always happiness
also our world becomes peace.

World Healing ~ World Peace 2020

A retired banker, C. S. P. Shrivastava studied Sanskrit, English and Psychology (Patna University). He is a sportsman with an understanding of world literature and human values. He has been writing Hindi and English poems for a long time. He views his poems as a process of being natural, a continuous effort to understand the intricacies of the human psyche and nature.

World Healing ~ World Peace 2020

Healing, Peace – The Solute

Peace no uncanny
Cliché
And no
Abyss
Roots are all fold -
Expansionism,
Racism, Religion
And sundry -
Those, crucify the
World Peace
The humanity that
Bled
Strove for
And
Attained the flow
Such names aren't
Low
Let's try to Glow
With head in
Pride
To Peace
Brotherhood be
The destined
And stride.

World Healing ~ World Peace 2020

Maria do Sameiro Barroso is a Portuguese medical doctor, a multi-lingual poet, translator, essayist and medical historian. She has authored over 40 poetry books, which were published in several countries. Her poems are translated in over 20 languages. She was awarded, among other recognitions, the prize, "Prayer for Saint Teresa" in Gjakovë, Kosovo in 2019.

Hope

Endless dreams, the purple heaven,
a bird across my face,
your heart a wonder,
the miracles of the world
unfolding light
while men strive to live
in the shelters of peace.
Could they breathe, overcoming
believes, limits, boundaries?
Could they breathe,
setting aside excessive
ambition and greed?
Earth corrodes skeletons.
Let men grow
just to enjoy the splendor of life,
the blue heavens,
the flowers of the night,
or the endless loving hands,
laying deep,
in the greenest valleys of the earth.

World Healing ~ World Peace 2020

Born in 1985 in Odisha, Abhilash Mishra, presently works as the Senior Branch Manager of the Bank of India in Bhubaneswar. He is an aspiring writer and poet, whose hobbies include reading books, manga, comics, and content on history and mythology, and sketching. [. . .]

https://www.facebook.com/abhilash.mishra.31

Miss Peace

She came as a breath
Of Freshest air.
If only I had time
To Spare.

Caught up in the
Din of the day.
Sweet nothings
I could scant play.

Her touch was lovely,
And yet fleeting.
Was stuck with my job
And some meeting.

Sad that one so dear
Is a guest.
Wish with me she
Would forever nest.

Will clean my Desk,
I've made up my Mind.
I'll break free of the
Routine grind.

Will pack my bags
And dump in a carriage.
Will seek her soothing
Hand in marriage.

Will get to compose
A masterpiece.
When I get to Wed
My muse, Miss Peace.

Chandra Shekar Pendoti is from the Mallapur village in Mandal Indalwai, Dist. Nizamabad Telangana State. He is working as a Post Graduate Teacher of English in the Telangana State's Model School-Nandipet Nizamabad. He has published several poems. He is one of the authors of the *Gurukul Mains English Language and Literature* book, which is published by the Telugu Akademie, Govt. of Telangana Hyderabad. [. . .]

An Epistle from the Almighty

Dear man!
I bless you with graceful garden
But you made it thyself burden.
Handle your life carefully
By steering it wonderfully.

Life grants invaluable gifts
Lift it yourself with numerous guts.
Make thy life haven
As if you were in heaven.

Shun all immaterial pieces
That are obtainable in the world masses.
Not to run after worthless money
Which imposes deep wounds many.

Make thy life devotionally
Not to lead it emotionally.
Disconnect all trivial emotions
So that thou get promotions.

Innumerable emotions are hidden
Not to pour them in heart with more burden.
All mankind hath emotions
Not to perish them with thy evil emotions.

Peace blooms in pious minds
Which make the world blooming Buds.
Nurture the nature as if you were brothers
Instead grabbing sources from others.

Lo! Dear man!
Thou live only once
Not to make it into menace
With your evil attitude
Mold it thyself altitude.
Shower compassion on fellow beings
Live life as brotherly human beings.
Adieu!!!

World Healing ~ World Peace 2020

The newest collection by Martina Reisz Newberry, *Blues for French Roast with Chicory* is due for publication from Deerbrook Editions in late fall, 2019. Her latest book, *Never Completely Awake* is available from the same publisher. Her literary work has been widely published in the U.S. and abroad. She lives in Los Angeles with her husband, Brian Newberry, a Media Creative.

World Healing ~ World Peace 2020

Clouds Like Boxcars

To stay sane, I research and pore
over the small things:
a chipped fingernail,
an odd-colored feather gracing the ground,
an unidentifiable spot on the kitchen floor,
a television show,
a book of crosswords.

Around my diversions, the wars continue.
They blend into each other
like creeks into lakes into rivers into oceans–
one immeasurable ocean–
unending tides of death, ineloquent battles
in defense of nothing we can remember.

Something, someone is always looking
for a new place to send someone else
to fight and die.
The endless ocean reflects heartbroken stars,
a morose moon–white as bone–
clouds like boxcars rolling and rolling,
stopping only to pick up more detritus,
more compromised air,
stopping only to deliver all of it
over an aching land.

None of us has to be told to be still anymore.
Our thoughts, the static of our consciences
simmers inside our brains.
We watch the skies for that specter of peace,
a summer of love, and still . . . and still . . .

When did the gods decide
that things were too easy for us?
When did our torpid breezes turn to strong winds
that howl and stumble below the canyons? *
No matter. The wars–the one war, the only war, goes on.

World Healing ~ World Peace 2020

We live inside our own dreams,
sorting particles of what we believe is right
from larger particles of what it takes to be happy.
We falter as we stand
on the foundations of our own souls.
Our bodies are haunted by the tough touch of time.

What will happen? We ask ourselves.
What will happen? We ask our loved ones.
What will happen? We ask the craters of the moon.
What will happen? We ask our fathers and brothers.
                    (Our mothers always knew).

Chthonic answers flood the world, won't let go
and chthonic spirits continue to watch and whisper.
There will be wars they say, *and rumors of war.*
I say I am aware. I know. I care. What about you?

My answer is always the same:
To stay sane, I research and pore over the small things:
a chipped fingernail,
an odd-colored feather gracing the ground,
an unidentifiable spot on the kitchen floor,
a television show,
a book of crosswords.

Hold steady, I say.

*R.I.P. Larry Kramer

Pushmaotee Subrun, born in Mauritius, pursued her higher studies at the Delhi University and has since been an educator in Mauritius and Zimbabwe. She completed her PGCE in Mauritius. After retirement, she became a member of the Council of the University of Mauritius. She is currently an editor at the Ministry of Arts and Culture. [. . .]

World Healing, World Peace 2020

World Healing to bring about World Peace
Can be a possibility with global armistice.
As it is, there are so many disparities,
With wealth and power imbalance,
Diversity in culture,
Religion in variety of procedure,
Being at war with each other, perpetually
All fragilizing global peace incessantly.

However, the basic pillar of our society, religion
Can bring about much desired change, with inculcation
Of the essence of spirituality for overall healing and peace.
The Holy Scriptures, full of the nectar of bliss,
Love, hope and faith, summum bonum preach,
Self-realization, morality, inner peace,
If made a priority, will mold the young minds certainly,
Into rational beings, lessen egocentric conflicts definitely.

Parental guidance is crucial, to inculcate discipline,
Not pampering children with latest mobiles,
Or violent electronic games.
The media can influence with peace propagating programs.
Besides, schools' curriculum should be revised,
Lessons on moral values and more activities devise,
Songs, poetry writing, plays, debates, impromptu speeches
Or drawings, all sensitizing right conduct, to maintain peace.

For World Peace to reign, involvement of many nations,
Peace treaties, talks and prompt actions,
Despite varieties of parties and political factions,
By a gradual evolution
In most human institutions,
Dealing with dissentions,
World Peace is possible by diplomatic involvements,
Nay World Peace for citizens' betterment.

World Healing ~ World Peace 2020

For the entire human race, for peace, justice and equality,
There is dire need for economic security,
Energy security,
Physical environmental security,
Food security,
Border security,
And cyber security.
The 'human race will shine in grace' with total harmony.

In harmony, world healing therapy won't arise,
The more so with inculcation of qualities,
Like respect, forgiveness, tolerance of differences,
Of caste, colour and creed, and races,
Causing divisiveness. Instead, supporting righteousness,
Inviting positivity and confidence,
Forgetting negative memories,
Will boost harmony, healing and peace.

Vidya Shankar, a poet, writer, motivational speaker, and yoga enthusiast, residing in Chennai, India, has been in ELT for more than two decades. She has been contributing articles, poems and stories to international literary platforms. She has published a poetry book, and has been on the editorial team for three publications.

https://shanvidwinsalways.blogspot.com/

Uni-Verse

From the One to one, and one unto the One
The United, the Unified, a completion so perfect
A fullness that when taken in parts
Yet remains as full
For, what is a Whole without its myriad fragments
Or that ultimate perfection without its disturbing imperfections?
What is the supreme Infinite without the miniscule Finite
And the eternal without the briefness of life?
As in you, so in me
An acceptance that begins with I to evolve to we
To merge with the I again
Therein lies the secret of the Universe
The undaunted truth that is love
The breath of which echoes
'Shanthih! Shanthih! Shanthih!'

World Healing ~ World Peace 2020

Shareef Abdur-Rasheed, AKA Zakir Flo, was born and raised in BKLYN,NY. He has received his education in BKLYN COLLEGE. A spoken word / poetry artist and a socio-political commentator, he has been composing poetry since the 60s. He plays Percussion, Congas, Timbales, Jazz & Salsa. He has published a book, *Poetic Snacks 4 The Conscious Munchies*, and contributed to numerous anthologies. [. . .]

World Healing ~ World Peace 2020

fulfill

the *fitrah
nature cries when
peace deprived
such a vital component
to being alive
one would think
to establish peace
individually, collectively,
globally, instinct
given the vital part it plays
like breathing everyday
one would think
perhaps in haste
for surely this is not the case
in spite of humans peace crave
it eludes him, her too often from
cradle to grave
does that make sense?
not until one recollects
since Cain killed Abel
man's crave for violence
and it's ability to render peace
silent
as in not enough or absence of
so, on one hand man craves peace
north to south, east to west
cradle to grave
on the other remains a slave
to flesh weak
thus, we must remember mankind's
dilemma
the peace one desires bestowed
upon the soul from above
is the same source that created
the one ingredient that's needed
to attain peace, sustain peace
LOVE!

food4thought = education ~ *fitrah = your nature

World Healing ~ World Peace 2020

An instructor in the National Cadet Core, India, Nitusmita Saikia is a keen worshiper of literature. She is working presently in Jorhat Assam, India. As a young budding poetess, she has been adored by the World Society of Poetry. She writes in both English and her own regional language, Assamese. Being active in various online poetry groups and blogs, she has been writing for E-Magazines. [. . .]

The Bleeding Dawn

Burning everywhere,
scared of those red and yellow flowers,
Our dawn in the warm wrap of smoke
The strangle hold of murderous human soul
We lost our beloved home and family forever.

Love to smell raw fragrance of green & wild,
Never have seen it hurting anyone but
Satiated all with its occasional treats,
Then why?
Why the sacrifice for your sake?
Why the foolery for fistful paper cakes!

Amazon was my nest
the garden! That has turned into a grave,
Now we don't hear it singing
Day and night in remorse for the terror,
we Amazonians are bleeding,
Human! you are the best beast we knew,
Each instant we are cursing only you.

We want,
No war no crime or nor bribe
Worshiping the mother nature
We are because it gives us life.
Then Why this power projection!
Was there any need for such destruction?

Our peace must be a threat,
A danger to your vanity,
Is there anyone who cries for my dead mother,
For my brother; for my dead friend ever?
Fighting alone here with a red and yellow flower,
No one knows why did it bloom,
But it has finished our world; our home shattered till doom.

World Healing ~ World Peace 2020

Anthony Arnold was born in Tampa and raised by his grandmother in a little town called Quincy in the Florida panhandle. He wrote his first piece in the third grade and fell in love with writing ever since that moment; writing has become a comfort and a mainstay to keep him focused.

Imagine

Imagine if you will
A world without strife,
A place without hatred, without racism
Can you see it?

War ceases to exist
Bombs are turned into plowshares
Where all live in harmony
And no words are spoken in anger

Only peace

Where Gandhi, King, and Malcolm X still lived
The Brothers Kennedy were just old men
Medgar Evers just walked into his house
Rosa parks never had to worry about the back of the bus

Imagine if you can
A world the way God intended
Where we all treated each other the way we wanted to be treated

Like human beings

"Do unto others as you would have them do unto you." (Matthew 7:12)

Boguslawa Chwierut was born in Czaniec, Poland. From 1990 on, she has lived in Libiąż. She is a writer from the needs of her heart for all those who love poetry. She is a culture animator and a lover of tradition. Since 2014, she has been a member of the groups "Cumulus" and "Academy of Words". [. . .]

World Healing ~ World Peace 2020

Ziemia Umiera

patrzę na umierającą ziemię
która ciężko oddycha
zniknęły kwiaty i zieleń
zostały na płycie wyobraźni
rozety mieczyków
fontanny róż
piwonie skłaniające się do pocałunku
malwy lewkonie irysy
iluminacje barw
w letnim poranku
umierają
z zachodem łamiąc łodygi
pośród zbitych brył
modlitwa poranna o deszcz
rozświetla dłonie
życie jak na pustyni
roztopione jak żółty ser
wiatrem i pod wiatr
rozlewają się szarość po ogrodzie
płynna zorza spływa na suchą trawę
wsiąknięta zachłannie przez otchłań
kruszy się pod butami
ziemia jak kamień
mój Boże
czuję się jak z wyrokiem

The Earth Is Dying

I look at the dying Earth
that breathes heavily
the flowers and greenery have disappeared
they've remained on the board of imagination
rosettes of gladioli
fountains of roses
peonies prone to kissing
mallows gillyflowers irises
illuminations of colour
in the summer morning
die
with the sunset breaking stalks
among amalgamated heaps
a morning prayer for rain
lights up hands
life like in the dessert
melted like yellow cheese
with the wind and against the wind
spills grey in the garden
liquid dawn flows onto dry grass
soaked greedily by the void
crumbles beneath our feet
Earth like stone
my God!
I feel like I've a sentence

World Healing ~ World Peace 2020

Rohini Kumar Behera is Deputy Secretary General of the World Union of Poets. Italy W.I.P. and Nigeria awarded him the "World Icon of Peace, Epitome of Humanity", "Ambassador of Peace"; H.P.A.W., Ghana appointed him as the "Ambassador of Humanity" and "Manager of Prince Art World". He is bestowed with a recognition as the "World Featured Poet" by PENTASI B. [. . .]

Peace Sublime

We want peace to reign
Let it flow like a stream
Into hearts of humanity
Blow trumpet of charity
Let peace be in Mankind
Peace is always imperative
Let not peace turn into pieces.

Eddies of tears will cease
Only gala smile will shine
Splendid peace may prevail
May tranquility be the slogan
Which surely sweep and reign
Along unending torrent upon
Blow the grandeur of heaven.

World Healing ~ World Peace 2020

Lennart Lundh is a poet, short-fiction writer, historian, and photographer. His work has appeared internationally since 1965. Following his service in Vietnam with the Navy's Amphibious Ready Group Bravo, Mr. Lundh was discharged as a conscientious objector.

Photos Taken in Evidence on the Streets of Two Capitals

Exhibit A, October 1967

The park is crowded, but all eyes are on a woman, seventeen, still in high school, she and the flower held as offering and option in her outstretched hands already a threat to those in power, enough that men at most two or three years her senior form a line to block her yet lean away as if the flower could kill, could somehow erase their crisp, green uniforms and ill-fitting steel helmets, could beat their rifles with fixed bayonets into things of real use and value. Having placed the potent flower in a rifle's barrel, knowing it can never stop lead on its own, she steps back, gaze unfaltering, spreads her arms wide as though presenting a sister's embrace, as if preparing to welcome bullet or blade, opening her life to welcome what comes next.

Exhibit B, February 1968

These streets are emptier, a calm space in the fighting occupied by soldiers watching the scene unfolding, a man in his later thirties, an officer in flak vest and stained fatigues, with a pistol in his outstretched right hand shining beneath the hot sun, the lines drawing all eyes along the short barrel to another, barely younger man, hands bound, shirt and short pants muddied by dust and fear, who grimaces, shuts his eyes tight, leans his head away from the bullet that will arrive by the time the next, post mortem frame is taken and he sprawls gracelessly on concrete. Having carried out the sentence, the first man holsters his pistol, turns, and moves on to the next act of war.

World Healing ~ World Peace 2020

Kerry Brackett is a poet and scholar who uses hip-hop and jazz influences for his poetry. He is the author of a few poetry chapbooks, including the upcoming *Surviving Myself*. He is currently teaching English at Miles College and is a doctoral student in the Humanities & Culture division at the Union Institute & University.

World Healing ~ World Peace 2020

Imagine

I heard Jimi said it best,
"When the power of love overcomes
The love of power, the world will know peace."
Can you imagine
A world without walls or boundaries
Where neighbors can shake hands?
Think of a world where you left Tennessee to
Go to Toronto to ask for some maple syrup
For your fresh pancakes.

Can you imagine
A world that forgot about war?
The definition of a foe would disappear
And replaced with that of a friend.
A society that wouldn't know what a gun was
Unless they saw it on the History channel.
No more violence, just natural causes
As souls gently escape in the breeze
While families mourn with more peace and tranquility.

Can you imagine
A world without greed?
Every dollar would be treated as a tumbleweed
Amongst the plains of civilization.
Food and fellowship would be more valuable
As the one with the most love become the richest.
No tricks for the trade
Everybody will get paid
All with a simple handshake.
Imagine.

Rickey K. Hood was born in Charlotte, NC. He is an award-winning poet, essayist and a playwright whose work has been published both nationally and abroad. He has earned his Bachelors of Arts degree in Religious Studies from The University of North Carolina at Charlotte in 2004. He now resides in the D.C. metro area.

World Healing ~ World Peace 2020

I Heard God Laughing

While sitting in the park
I heard the laughter of children
Loud and wonder sounding
As rain on withering leaves
And it was then I understood
That it was God I heard laughing.

The soft still voice in the wind
Broke forth in a belly shaking laugh
Filling the air with a pure, unconditional joy
A good belly laugh not filled with wrath,
Vengeance, punishments or judgments

I was surprised to hear that it was
Not a "look at man's foolishness" laugh
Or, God is laughing at us, laugh
But instead, God is laughing with us
Enjoying the joy of the day

I now can hear that God is a happy God
Whose laughter rains down
Through the voice of children
Upon a parched earth
Cooling and refreshing it with life

We all have heard the laughter of children
But how many of us
Has ever heard the laughter of God?

World Healing ~ World Peace 2020

Thaddeus Hutyra (known also as Tadeusz Hutyra) was born in Poland where he attended schools and begun to study at the prestigious Jagiellonian University of Cracow. Shortly afterwards, before a state of emergency was announced by the communist regime on the 13th of December 1981, he left Poland in search of a better life abroad. [. . .]

World Healing ~ World Peace 2020

The Thinker

An old man with long grey hair and a grey beard
Bending over a book bound with goat skin
In his starry mind, the paths of the wise men
Whose works he had already read thoroughly.

Eureka! * . . . Cogito ergo sum ** . . . Wisdoms of predecessors
Brilliantly glow in the universe of his mind
Not as a directive but as navigational hints
For in his opinion there is no ultimate truth.

He picked up his pen, leaned over his book
"Man!" – He wrote. "No philosophy or dogma
Are the definitive truth. They are but your nourishment."

"Man!" He continued, "They are only molecules
like the Higgs boson enabling you to discover yourself
in the spirit of freedom, in which you are an eagle in its skies.

So . . . Don't be too serious with your philosophy
Don't be too serious with your religious views
We all are roses of Jericho, sent by the winds
To four points of the world, then resurrecting
Having new lives, time upon time, upon time.

World healing is you and me, all of us
Taking into our hands precious stones of peace
And holding them as a reminder the world is us."

"Man!" – Exclaimed the thinker in the end
"Be the cosmic rays of healing
Here on this star ship called Earth
Take care of you, of us all, be angels of Earth
For we all are a family, one called humankind!"

World Healing ~ World Peace 2020

"Man!" – Let's open our hearts, let's heal the world
Let's free our minds, have fun, enrich ourselves with freedoms
May the lights of peace, lights of healing light us forever
And be our eternal way of life, so help us, God!

* "Eureka" comes from the Ancient Greek word εὕρηκα heúrēka, meaning "I found (it)", an exclamation attributed to the Ancient Greek mathematician and inventor Archimedes.
** "Cogito, ergo sum" is a Latin philosophical proposition coined by the philosopher René Descartes, which is usually translated into English as "I think, therefore I am".

Eliza Segiet graduated with a Master's Degree in Philosophy. The author's poem, "Questions" won the title of the International Publication of the Year (2017) by Spillwords Press. Her poem, "Sea of Mists" won the title of the International Publication of the Year (2018) by Spillwords Press.

Guidance

If in the universe
governed tolerance,
there would be no need
for the cry of despair after loss.

We are born in different spaces,
on one aqueduct of life.
Do some have to be connected by hate?

It is worth understanding
that death
should not be ruled by humans,
but rather time
that imperceptibly
leads us through the staff of life.

After all, breath given to us
is the beginning and the end
- of everything.

It's enough
- just simply -
for a human
to understand a Human.

If in the universe
tolerance was the guidance . . .

Translated by Artur Komoter

World Healing ~ World Peace 2020

Danuta Błaszak was born in Warsaw, Poland, and lives with her family in Orlando, Florida. She studied the theory of shape and the infinitely dimensional spaces in the Department of Mathematics at Warsaw University. She has completed her postgraduate studies in journalism. She is the editor-in-chief of the Miasto Literatów 2000 ++. [. . .]

pilot and a girl, II

you ask me Danuska why I smoke a hundred cigarettes a day
this is how it started

I was a child
they killed the Warsaw uprising and my sister and I
were separated from our parents in the Pruszkow camp
a kind soul took us away on a wagon filled with dead bodies

my sister and I ran as fast as we could
she was little, I not much older than her
we fell asleep cuddled

in a cargo car on a dead-end railroad in the woods
we woke up locked inside
listening to the heavy breathing of the train
trapped with no food or water

we were saved by bombs
we escaped through a hole in the roof
the locomotive breathed heavily in the ditch

I tried to earn money to buy food
a field cook found me
old Wasilenko fed me
I felt guilty
my sister died of starvation

the cook rolled my first cigarette

later in a flat taken over from a German
I played with a toy car
the cook along with other Bolsheviks died in the war

I learned how to smoke

Translated by Anna Sledziewska-Bolinska

World Healing ~ World Peace 2020

Anna Maria Mickiewicz is a poet, writer and editor who writes both in Polish and in English. Anna moved to California, and then to London, where she has lived for many years. She edits the annual literary magazine, *Pamiętnik Literacki* (*The Literary Memoir*), and *Contemporary Writers of Poland* (USA). She is a member of English Pen. [. . .]

They Were Not the Ones

They were not the ones

Who ordered the trees to be silent

Who gagged the spring birds

They stand in the glow of the rising sun

Worrying about what will happen

Christena Williams is a Jamaican award-winning author, performer, youth volunteer and an ICPI cultural ambassador. She holds a B.A. degree (Honors) in History (major) and Philosophy (minor) from The University of the West Indies. Her book, *Pearls Among Stones* has been recognized with the Prime Minister's National Youth Awards for Excellence in Arts and Culture.

World Healing ~ World Peace 2020

Peace and Healing

Re-plant the trees
Say No to GMO
Preserve our History and Heritage
Preserve our oceans, rivers and our most precious sacred spaces
Preserve life as we may never know the future
Keep our environment clean
Respect our elders
Keep our women, elders, disable and babies safe
Respect our safe spaces
Respect people no matter of their creed, skin tone, political affiliations
Peace is respect
Peace is truth
Peace is in our mind, souls, body and heart
So why not exercise it
When will we realize that mother earth is to be respected
and not demoralize by our greed?
When will we take accountability of our destructive actions
that have led to global warming?
When will we stop blaming God for our own wickedness against humanity?
When will we love each other as we truly love ourselves?
When will we realize that we are all suffering from pain and aches
and we need each other?
When will realize that no man stands alone in the face of adversity?
When will we realize that unity is indeed our strength and our weapon?
Not bullets, bombs and man-made diseases
When will we forge our greatest assets: people,
and build a greater future for our generations to come?
Healing begins when you know you are hurting
Healing begins when we are ready to speak and cry
Healing begins when we are ready to forgive
Healing begins when we are ready to have that discussion
Healing begins when we are ready to be vulnerable
that we wear our pain like a canvas
Healing begins when you have forgiven yourself
Healing begins when nothing else is left but Healing
Healing begins with you.

World Healing ~ World Peace 2020

Smruti Ranjan Mohanty, O.F.S, son of Raj Kishore and Shantilata, is a multilingual poet, an essayist and a writer. His write-ups are published in newspapers and in various widely acclaimed national and international magazines, journals and anthologies.

smrutiweb.wordpress.com

World Healing ~ World Peace 2020

From This Side of the Wall

From this side
I am stretching my hands,
from that side, you come forward.
Give me your hand,
we will walk hand in hand
on the path of peace and prosperity
and rewrite the history of mankind.

Neither you know me, nor I know you.
Why so much of hatred and jealousy.
Nothing is common between you and me
except we share the same feelings
to flower and flourish and live
a beautiful life in peace and amity.

I am opening my heart, you open yours,
only a single heart beating for the sake of humanity and the victory of life and love,
nothing in between you and me except our make belief man-made identity

Open your eyes, I am opening mine.

Look at history, written in the blood of fallen martyrs, the battles and wars
fought over the years to satisfy a few, their ego, greed and vanity.

Let us open the closed window to look at each other and see
the sad panorama of human woes and listen to the poignant tales of many,
the voice of their wounded hearts and shattered dreams.

My friend! we have every right to dream a better tomorrow,
where reign supreme peace, truth and love, no frontier and ego
to jealously guard, a just world order, where justice is never denied,
and equal opportunity for all irrespective of region, religion,
caste, creed and colour

World Healing ~ World Peace 2020

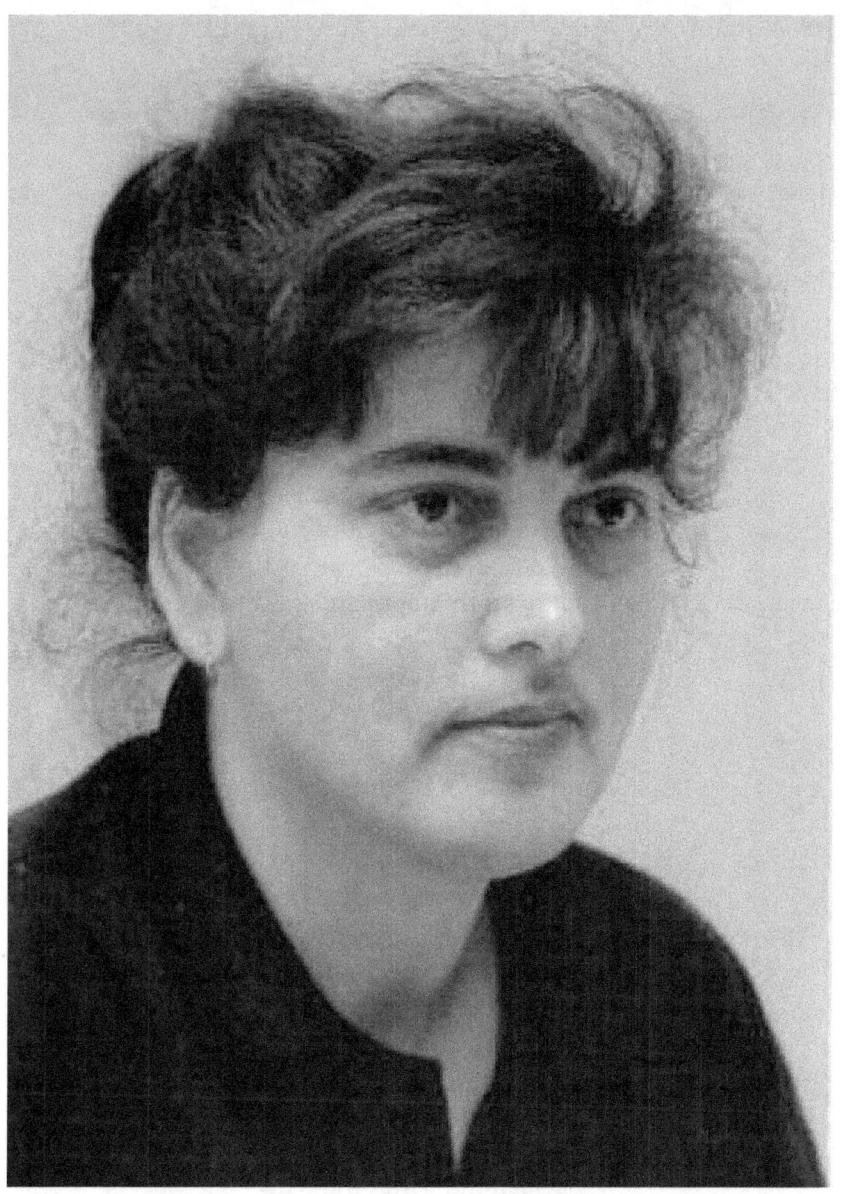

Born in 1962, Snežana Šolkotović is a teacher. Writing is her hobby. She has published 16 poetry books and stories for children and adults. A number of her poems and stories have been featured in numerous national and international anthologies, collections and journals. She has won prestigious awards at domestic and international competitions.

World Healing ~ World Peace 2020

JA ŽELIM SAMO MIR . . .

Svaki trenutak je obojen pretnjom
zveckanjem oružja, pozivom na krvavi pir,
dan se gubi sa nekom pometnjom,
a ja želim, ljudi, samo MIR.

Smrt na svakom koraku vreba
trpeljivosti je sve manje,
malo više smeha i sreće treba
ljubav među ljudima i razumevanje.

Pružite ruku prijateljstva svima
topao osmeh, pokažite dobru volju,
ma koliko razlika na ovom svetu ima
mir čini čuda i budnućnost bolju.

Nije bitna boja kože,
na kojoj se strani sveta živi,
Mir je ono što sve spajati može,
svojim duginim bojama da zadivi.

Nije bitan jezik kojim se govori,
mudrost je stara svima odavno znana,
za mir treba svako da se bori
njen ključ je među nama.

Pustite goluba da poleti
grančicu mira neka svetom podeli,
malo je potrebno nekog voleti
dovoljno je samo da se mir želi . . .
A ja želim samo mir . . .

World Healing ~ World Peace 2020

I Only Want Peace

Each moment is colored with the threat,
Rattling weapons and the calling of the bloody revel,
The day is being lost with some kind of confusion,
And people, all I want is PEACE.

Death lurks on every corner,
The span of tolerance is shorter,
Laughter and happiness are needed more,
Love and understanding furthermore.

Give a hand of friendship to everyone,
Show a warm smile and good will,
No matter how many differences are there in this world,
Peace makes miracles and the future improved.

The color of the skin is unimportant,
And living in any part of the world,
Peace can connect anything,
With its rainbow colors that are astonishing.

The spoken language is irrelevant,
Ancient wisdom known by everyone,
Everybody should fight for the peace,
Its key should be released . . .

Let the pigeon out to fly,
The twig of peace to share worldwide,
It takes so little to love someone,
Wishing the peace is all it takes
To become one . . .
And all I want is PEACE.

B. S. Tyagi comes from India. He writes in both Hindi and English. He has several books of fiction and non-fiction to his credit. His poems have been included in several anthologies. He writes short stories which regularly appear in national and international literary magazines. His reviews have appeared in national magazines across the country. He has translated four poetry books.

To an Autumn Leaf

(1)

Leaf- dry, pale, red and brown
    Bare big tree stands in the yard,
A lone bird stares up and down,
    Everything sad, serene and hard,
On my life autumn comes to stay like a guard.

(2)

In icy winds all boughs sigh and sway
    Far and wide sharp frost covers the grounds,
Tyrant times ever keep all joys at bay,
    Many hard blows chase me like the hounds,
Dreams writhe around lying low with murmuring sounds.

(3)

No leaf, no flower, no sunshine
    No chirping or cooing, singing heart,
What can a despairing heart pine?
    Misfortunes ever been a life's part,
All alone I've to bear myself the burden of my cart.

(4)

O, leaf in this fall thou art not alone
    Chilly winds have pierced through me,
Melodies once filled me with joy gone,
    Chilling darkness all around I can see,
All sweet dreams and desires are bidden to flee.

World Healing ~ World Peace 2020

(5)

Like me thou in prime lying so helpless
    Thrown by the gales of time on sodden grass,
Like me thou burnt-out and breathless,
    Angry time has taken away all my life's brass,
Lovely words and songs lying like shreds of broken glass.

(6)

Like me thou art abandoned for no reason
    Drained of all strength, vigor and vitality,
Glimmer and youthful hope of the season,
    Like me thou slowly suffering from fragility,
Gone forever sweetness of love, longing and hilarity.

(7)

Like me thou badly failed to ravel life out
    So dragged heavy dark days and nights on,
Like me thou fallen and tasted the bitter rout,
    And couldn't see golden sunbeams of dawn,
The river of time keeps flowing freely past on and on.

(8)

Autumn leaf, thou art far and far better
    Thou can feel and bathe in the moon-light,
Soothing and balmy freeing thou from fetor,
    Thou can feel breezy, brimming and bright,
Thou may enjoy with the mighty wind a hilarious flight.

(9)

Don't grieve dear, thou art not that worse
    Lying beneath thy own thick and old tree,
I can't do nothing but scribble a small verse,
    Under the soils thou have live seeds free,
At the approaching of the East wind they'll be on a spree.

World Healing ~ World Peace 2020

(10)

For sure here thou will decay and be dead
    Afterwards many blossoms spring to life,
And will live through them in many a bed,
    Prostrate with grief, and empty cup of life,
 Oh me! Never more will rise up in this unequal strife.

(11)

In my solitary yard old, rough and bare tree
    Bursting with burnt ochre blossoms galore,
Spring splashing all colors and joy spilling free,
    Even the tiniest bough will remain no bore,
Alas! For feasting my eyes on pristine beauty I'll be no more.

Aabha Rosy Vatsa is a published author, poet, writer, blogger and former teacher. She has published twelve poetry books, one travelogue, one short story collection and edited a children's poetry anthology. Her poems have been published in international ezines. She believes in Karma philosophy.

A Beacon

O, be a beacon of light
Do your bit to sway the sorry plight
Dance like a woman possessed
Raise matters not addressed

Let the light enlighten one and all
Gather wisdom as you scale the wall
Let the glitter not ever dim
Make sure the chances of worry are slim

Embrace all and express love
Let worry fly over and above
Alight along this delightful journey
Spread sweetness like pure honey

Let the path be lit with golden lights
Look out for commendable sights
The dance and frolic will come your way
Hold your friend captive, don't let her sway

Drive away the lengthening shadows
Breeze in lush green meadows
Let your life be lived worthwhile
Come on, be an exemplary beacon, smile.

Jason Constantine Ford is from Perth, Australia. He has over a hundred publications of poetry and fiction in various literary magazines, ezines and journals from around the world. Edgar Alan Poe and William Blake are his main influences for poetry. Phillip K. Dick is his main influence for fiction.

A White Dove

In early hours of a morning just begun,
A form of freedom reigns without a single speck.
From out of clouds, a dove appears below the sun
Transcending worthless values creatures wreck.
Although shadows of vice are spread across the land,
A single dove remains immune to what is bland
Or what is false as she is passing through
The air of human lies as fading residue.
Not a single word of hate can penetrate
The flight of wings resisting falsity
As she aligns herself with values straight
Across a path imbued with clarity.
High above the world, she avoids the stain
Of lies which plague the creatures who are vain.

Maritza Martínez Mejía is a mother, an educator, a bilingual author and translator. She has founded the Luz del Mes Tri-Anthology and the Proyecto de Escritura Luz del mes. She is the recipient of the Crystal Apple Award 2006, VCB Poetry 2015, and the Latino Book Awards 2016. Maritza writes to inspire others to be better persons.

www.luzdelmes.com

Mother Earth Talks

As the winds roared and furiously destroyed everything on its way,
the Earth talks to me,

    "You see the signs,
    Hear my fury,
    But you don't listen.

    You are so fragile,
    I do not want to hurt you,
    But you don't act.

    Recycle, reuse, and reduce
    You know it,
    You know it, but you don't do it!

    Do not cut down trees, nor divert rivers,
    You know it,
    You know it, but you don't do it!

    Avoid the consumption of plastics,
    You know it,
    You know it, but you don't do it!

    Hypocrites! If you know how to interpret the climate,
    Why do not interpret the signs of the present time?"

Deep silence arrived while the eyes of the storm passed by . . .

World Healing ~ World Peace 2020

Born in 1970, Hussein Habasch is a poet from Afrin, Kurdistan and lives in Bonn, Germany. Kurdish and Arabic are his literary languages. Some of his poems have been translated to many languages, including English, German, Spanish, French, Chinese, Turkish, Persian, Albanian, Uzbek, Russian, and Romanian. He wrote a large number of books, and a selection of his poems have been published in numerous international poetry anthologies. [. . .]

The Difference Between You and Me

The difference between you and me
Is that you sit cross-legged
Leisurely savouring your glass of wine
While I wrap myself around myself
As I gulp from the glass of pain at the hospital.
You post the photo of your ninety something mother on Facebook,
Still in her prime!
And I remember the complexions of my seventy something mother,
With all her wrinkles!
You see her every day and place a peck on her cheeks
Whereas I have seen her only twice in twenty-two years
I kiss her photo every day in longing.
God bless our mothers!
You follow all football matches
You laugh, comment, cheer and support this team against that one
While I follow all the agonies of my people in Afrin
I weep, despond, curse and grieve for what has befallen them.
Your sister has a splendid house in the city center
Whilst my two sisters are vagrants, homeless and vagabonds,
A family from Ghouta occupied the house of one,
And a family from Qalamun occupied the house of the other.
You sit with your only brother
And debate how to split your father's vast legacy
While I worry about the affairs of my brothers, exiled and fleeing,
scattered around the globe,
I have no means to reunite them and to bring them to safety.
Your country is Germany
My country is Kurdistan
Two worlds apart
Germany is flourishing and growing at each moment and minute
While Kurdistan is slaughtered and murdered at each moment and second.
Your country is exporting Leopard tanks to kill what breath was left
in the lungs of my country!

And my compatriots who miraculously survived the killing machine
Are applying in their scores for asylum at your country.
You were born with a golden spoon in your mouth
And I was born with a poison challis in my mouth.
This is only a drop of an ocean of differences between you and me
I shall not go on unfolding the pain that adjoined me as a twin since birth
Despite the differences you see between us
I fully understand why you celebrate life
I never understand why I despair of it!

Translated by Hishyar Abid

Born in Leon Guanajuato, Mexico on April 21, 1977, Fernando Martinez Alderete is a writer, poet, theater actor, and radio producer. His poems were published in 63 anthologies in thirteen countries around the world, and he is the author of two books, one of poetry and another of short stories.

Heal in Peace

Over time secrets are discovered,
hidden words in the pores of Man;
beauty in the world also hurts,
the most beautiful works of art in the world
they are created in a state of pain of intense being.

Peace is the medicine that heals the soul,
the restorative balm of the earth,
but they always threaten fear and war;
respecting freedom the sorrows end,
Building the joy of living happily.

Only love and peace will heal the universe,
but we must kill the fatal selfishness,
seize the useless racism to alleviate hate,
seek justice with eternal serenity,
sing hymns of forgiveness among brothers.

The illusion of a beginning of peace must be created,
the excitement of a new era of light must be turned on,
the sadness of the absent who did not learn, banish it,
the happiness of those present enjoy it,
the prosperity of the peoples allows it.

Rubab Abdullah, now a citizen of the United States, was born in Dhaka, Bangladesh. She has her higher education from the University of Dhaka. She is a published poet whose work has appeared in many anthologies and newspapers in both, Bangladesh and the USA. [. . .]

https://www.facebook.com/ruwwad.sabri

Love Heals

The far greater be
Our sense of love
It endows the hue to nature
The blue sky seems deific
At the crack of dawn
As a hope to continue breathing.

The green grass looks greener
The rustling sounds of dry leaves
Play a symphony to anyone's ears.

Love heals a wounded heart
So too it shares the pleasure of life,
Living in bliss or catastrophe
The feeling deepens the longing for prayers.

Kay Salady is a writer and an advocate for peace. She is based in the Seattle area. She has been a featured author in several online magazines directed towards non-violence, and has joyfully taken part in anthologies for causes such as breast cancer awareness and world peace.

kaysalady.wordpress.com

To Break the Silence

Imprisoned by the silence
this loneliness has wrought
I sit here in the shadows
shuffling through each thought
that echoes down the halls
of isolation that I share
with other kindred spirits
who have had too much to bear

So deep within the shadows
I now listen for the words
I have sent into these halls
but there is nothing to be heard
for I am deafened by the silence
that hollowness has brought
I weep within the darkness
as I pray to find my thoughts

I place my mark upon this wall
to prove that I am here
and that you are not alone
with the cross you have to bear
There is screaming in the silence
when you can find no words
to reach beyond your walls
so that you can be heard

I am stabbed by your injustice
and inflicted with your pain
There is such a loss for words
when the world is so insane
We sit inside the silence
waiting for our words
while we stare at whitewashed walls
in this land of the absurd

World Healing ~ World Peace 2020

We fall upon our knees
with an ear to their closed doors
waiting very patiently
for those who won't do more
Then we listen very closely
for those who came before
to break the silence

Is there one here among us
with the fortitude to cope
who would knock at every door
with the urgency and hope
to crack man's hardened shell
so his inner child shines through
The only way to break the silence
is to show them what they do

World Healing ~ World Peace 2020

Dr. Tzemin Ition Tsai (蔡澤民博士) was born in 1957 in Taiwan, the Republic of China. He holds a Ph.D. in Chemical Engineering and is a professor at the Asia University. His literary creations, specializations and expertise focus on the description of nature, the anatomy of emotion and humanity.

https://www.facebook.com/tzemintsai

Poet, Adhesion in the Shadow of a Tree

The pine forest in front of the river bank was still deep
Pedestrians haunted in the woods
Pedestrians were blocked by the mountain again
It was a wild place
Spears and swords replaced the axiom arguments
I secretly hid in the shadow of the tree
Wrote it all on the bark
Before it was swallowed into the annual-rings
We built a home in the woods
The birds sang beside each other with joy
When our government set up a reservation for us
I walked around the stream to the edge of the forest
And gradually felt that fear was leaving us
I know
The bell of peace has never sounded smoothly
If my people can't walk into the polling station
If our children were not allowed to enter college
When I look back again
I would rather this is a trip in the deepest in our hearts
In the depths of the virgin forest
In the depths of our lives

World Healing ~ World Peace 2020

Dr. Su Jen Lin (林素珍博士) comes from Taiwan. She is a professor in the Department of Chinese of the National Changhua University of Education. With the dream of traveling around the world, she has been constantly writing about many of her touristic experiences.

https://www.facebook.com/SU JEN LIN

World Healing ~ World Peace 2020

I Stand up for What I Believe in

The best and most beautiful things in the world
can not be seen or even touched,
They must be felt with heart.
It's only with the heart that I can see rightly.

I'm not afraid of tomorrow
for I have seen yesterday and love today.
The value of life lies not length of days,
but in the use of I make of them.

I can!
Because I believe in myself.
A winner never quits.
Nothing is impossible to a willing heart.
I'll do my best,
And not have to worry about failure.

I believe that adversity is a good discipline.
Accept any failure and move on.
After a storm comes a calm.
Every cloud has a silver lining.

I see opportunities in every calamity.
Adversity successfully overcome is the highest glory.

Soma Bhowmik is the proprietor of S KAYS SOLUTION, an educator and a physiological counsellor. She has specialized in free lancing, content writing, blog writing, creative writing in English, Hindi and Bangla, contemporary art, painting on canvas and acting in short films. Being an ambitious woman, she is attached to the creative world as an artist and writer. [. . .]

https://www.facebook.com/profile.php?id=100008448431538

World Healing ~ World Peace 2020

A Thought

In this world of terror and violence
Let's sit back and think in silence
About our wishes and real desire
Who really think and do care
Then probably we will be able to decide
our own priorities keeping everything beside.

Life is simple ,life is short
Love , sympathy and empathy
Is what we have forgot
People do care
But don't dare to share
Everyone is engrossed in their own affairs

Teach your son to respect his mom and sis
Don't teach your daughter to be selfish
Help someone in case of need
Save not on your account
but on your good deeds.

Do forgive rather than punish
One day surely the violence will vanish.

Ushie James Obule is an author, a poet, a public and motivation speaker from Nigeria. He is a biochemist by profession.

World Peace

When wars and conflicts totally cease,
In our world, there shall be peace.
People must learn to get along,
Not blame others, for being wrong.
They fight for control, fight for land,
Some just need a helping hand.
We must rid ourselves of vanity,
And embrace peace, through humanity.
Wars make children so much tougher,
Lose their innocence, while they suffer.
We should fight for peace instead,
Love not war, we should spread and promote peace
for the interest and betterment of mankind.

World Healing ~ World Peace 2020

Christine Von Lossberg was the featured artist in the biggest visionary art shows in Los Angeles by Atlanta Gallery as well as in museums and art events in Germany, Hawaii, Italy, England, Holland, Canada and Mexico. She has face-painted over 3000 children around the world, and writes stories for them.

World Healing ~ World Peace 2020

The Peace Dream

A day as each day,
Everyone living in their fears
their uncertainties and joys
All the children that we are
inside all girls and boys,
One day the clouds made
funny things all over the world!
The world laughed and cheered!
As the world turned from day to night
The world had turned into black and white!
All breathing and heart beats together
Was it something in the weather?
Everyone slept and had the same dream!
When we opened our eyes it was the new bright magic colors!
The colors of wonder, the colors of peace!
The love we were made of everyone knew,
We all understood each other
We were one there was not me and you!
All friends, lovers, living in bliss
Instead of a handshake it was now the eternal kiss!
We all loved each other and could see the beauty of each soul,
Our hearts beat as One the love of our Divine
Creator in each heartbeat and breath of peace,
We all remembered the Peace dream and each
new baby knew it from the day they were born!
Peace was all there was, never no war!

World Healing ~ World Peace 2020

Hailing from Bekwarra, Cross River State, Egbung Elizabeth Omaku was born in Kano State, Nigeria on June 1st, 2000. She has completed her primary and secondary education in Kano, Nigeria, and is presently studying architecture at Hassan Usman Katsina Polytech in Katsina State.

World Healing ~ World Peace 2020

Peace

What else could it be

What should my request be

What could cause me to flee

disagreeing with all parts of me

Harmony in absence of hostility and violence, lack of conflict,
freedom from fear of violence, more than a negotiating opportunity,
absence of negativity, all our wish

It stings our mind like a bee believing that we're sinking, we've kept thinking,
kept searching, writing until no ink was left in our pen just to find the missing piece of
what left us divided

As dark drew closer something dawn on me, how were we able to come this far,
what existed in the past that we might have killed or passed by without giving a lift

For just like the shadows of the night overtaken by daylight it was overtaken by us,
valour and fortitude are its wheels, it is not just an imagination I can feel it,
it can merge the nations, believe me

It is not just my dream please share in it, if we don't find it there's no thought of living

PEACE!

A lovely process, like an angel gradually changing opinions, like an ocean
slowly eroding old barriers, like a single builder quietly building new structures is peace,
it is expensive but worth the expense

It is a precious stone and its purest form should be found in the soul of the world
without digging deep, it is a kiss to an enemy, it is a sewing thread needed
in a war-torn world

Peace: a requirement for development

Peace: an index for measuring development either which way without its chaos,
because normalcy and life becomes Hobbessian: poor, nasty, brutish and short.

World Healing ~ World Peace 2020

Prepare for war if you want peace, war against all odds militating human
and collective wellbeing and improvement. The opposite of peace is not war
but deceitful peace camouflaging on the surface but ravishing away
the very fabric of pleasant livelihood in pretense.

Peace in Latin: pacem

In French, Paix

Arabic: Salam

Hausa: Salama

Yoruba: Alafia

Igbo: Udo

Galician: paz

Swedish: Fred

Swahili: Amani

Peace begins with a smile, the result of retaining your mind to process life peace
is rather than what you think it should be

For just like a broken bottle we are broken into pieces but we can still make peace
with our broken pieces for where there is love it doesn't exist, don't ask for an address
to it, it only lives in a body, a country without a missing part in silence

Imagine a place where love is abundant, where there is no cry of a baby heard
cause an enemy called war never pays visit, where colour doesn't matter,
no black no white (racism) when someone is without it others give
so through unity we all can live not kill for when the power of lover overcomes
the love of power the world will know peace exists

Lord, please hear my cry, give us an inner peace, the manifestation of
human compassion, inner peace so that the world peace may begin, give us peace,
not peace which passeth understanding but understanding that bringeth peace

World Healing ~ World Peace 2020

The world is in the end of history, full of the noise of superior civilization and space technology wrapped up in calculated peace but has totally lost the language of true serenity, love is what we need the purest form of a soul at peace it is

We cannot avoid peace by avoiding life, no way, but we can enjoy life by finding peace, looking for the way. There is no way to peace -peace is the way

World, have compassion, don't be selfish it only brings anguish; the world suffers from lack of peace when more people like you and I live without compassion that's nasty

Peace is daily like our daily meal, weekly like our weekly activities, monthly like our wages. Peace is its own reward and forever exists as long as the creator of the creatures exist

Even our existence and presence here to freely express our thoughts is a product and gift parceled with peace, someone close needs a peace cake please bake, it tastes sweeter but war, bitter

War is a crime; peace is a gift and you owe me one. Let there be PEACE.

Priya Unnikrishnan was born in Kerala, India, and resides now in Texas, USA. She writes poems and short stories in Malayalam, and has her work published in different magazines and newspapers. She has authored two books of poetry and one book of short stories. She has contributed to numerous publications with her poems, memories and stories.

https://www.facebook.com/priya.unnikrishnan.908

Peace by War

A few kids
deep in slumber
by the cold lake
with bullets in their hearts.

The earth laments
like the sting of a deep gash.
I raise my voice
seeking justice in law.

They uproot me and throw me aside
like an irrelevant weed.

The war for peace gets battle ready
with the white flag unfurled.

Translated by Ra Sh

Tanja Ajtic lives in Vancouver, Canada. Her poems and stories were published in fifty collections and / or books. In October 2018, KOS Belgrade published her first book of poetry, *The Contours of Love*, which was displayed at the 2018 Book Fair in Belgrade and the 2019 Book Fair in Toronto.

World Healing ~ World Peace 2020

A River

You who live near the river
You believe in images of little gods of love
in ancient Roman art
and Renaissance as well as a new era.
In a lovely little winged child entertained with
various jobs
you see them and speak like Socrates:
"I know I do not know anything!"
You say that the world is a property without a master
and that it is not known who its creator is?
You as a free thinker, neither good nor bad,
indifferent, but not powerless.
You see those beautiful children in the glare of the river
which flows for you into infinity and you enjoy.
You have a safe haven and enough air
to survive everything
in the air that can cause it
chemical changes and you can calculate them
only if you want.
You live in your own reflection of an image
and I believe you
that the world can be a nice place
if we look at ourselves.
Then everything is clear.

Otteri Selvakumar has simple dreams: today is better than to think and write about tomorrow. He has written poetry and short stories for many online magazines and newspapers. He has participated in over 50 international anthologies with his poem contributions.

The Noise

Night time
While waiting for silence
The moon is smiling in milk
It is a noise coming
When you think about what it is
The noise of dogs
Coming out of the side street
The noise of the night breaks
Missing in the noise of dogs
The search for peace
Yes, I am . . .
I woke up awake from a sleep
Looking for a return to sleep
But the noise of the dogs could not
In addition there is . . .

World Healing ~ World Peace 2020

Orbindu Ganga is an Indian post-graduate in sciences and the first recipient of the Dr. Mitra Augustine Gold Medal for academic excellence. He has authored a book, *Saudade*. He is a poet, content writer, painter, researcher and spiritual healer. He has published many poems, research papers and articles, and has completed several paintings.

http://mysignatureisauro.blogspot.com/?m=1

World Healing ~ World Peace 2020

Lighting a Candle of Hope

Misty fogs have fled
Along the coast of poles,
Tears started to flow
Promised never to dry,
Thinning along the edges
Shedding the wings to fly,
Slowly moving away from the sleet
Sauntering at her pace,
Welkin are devoid of nebulous
Scattered in parsimony,
Thoughts of sprinklers are in dreams
Seldom are they seen,
Rising is the drops
Sinking is the floaters.

Living long in a utopian world
Like the smiling arrows,
Deceiving many for long
Still holding the smile,
Years have gone
A very few wordings at times,
To evince the world
The atrocities of mankind,
Passing the baton
Many times, you failed,
Every time you promised
Letting us down with a smile,
For ages she has been waiting
For us to take a stand,
Many times, we never
Made an attempt,
As the siren rang
They played to the galleries,
Never did we question
The leaders,
They took us

World Healing ~ World Peace 2020

For a ride for ages,
Against the wriggles of witches
Many joined the bandwagon.

Young has a heart
Talking without fear,
Fewer battles have they seen
In the early hours seeing the mirror,
A little did they see
Blazing the crescendo across the globe,
Small fingers are lighting
The candle of hope,
Away from the glean
To make their voices felt,
Talking hard against the imposters
With a bleeding heart,
Forming a synergy across the globe
Spelling the beans to evince,
Slicing the words
To shunt the arrogance,
Spreading the language of peace
To heal the wounds of nature.

World Healing ~ World Peace 2020

Norbert Góra is a 29 year-old poet and writer from Poland. He is the author of more than 100 poems which have been published in poetry anthologies in the USA, the UK, in India, Nigeria, Kenya and Australia.

Peace Has Built This World

Humanity still forgets,
its memory is short
as the sum of our days,
it must be constantly made aware
that peace has built this world.

Wars took everything from us,
the walls of the houses
were cracking like hearts,
ashes instead of dreams,
despair replaced happiness.

Look at the horizon,
the black conflagration is coming,
the work of peace today
nobody appreciates,
but the blind civilization
will mention the Great Builder one day,
when another conflict reveals the foundation
that once made a beautiful and safe universe.

World Healing ~ World Peace 2020

Pankhuri Sinha is a bilingual poet and story writer, starting her first novel. She has two books of poems in English, *Dear Suzannah* and *Prison Talkies*, two collections of stories and four poetry books published in Hindi, and many more writings on both genres are lined up. She has won numerous prestigious national awards for her writings in Hindi. [. . .]

The Invisible War

With no soldiers
Not a single boot down
No enrollment
Just a reign of terror
Unspeakable terror
For certain people in town
People with other countries
Other languages
The other kind of look
People who walk the town
Somewhat more dilapidated
In times of such invisible wars
Such outbursts
Such outbreaks
People whose othering
Is slowly being completed
By this very war . . .

And the last class lecture
Has just explained
How the earth always remains
Calm and stable
In these parts of the world . . .

The last class has also divided
The world in these two halves
Of the breakable
And the unbreakable
The last class
Has also given
The explicit command
Of keeping them down . . .

Deema Mahmood is an Egyptian poet born in 1972. In 1993, she has earned a Bachelor's degree in Computer Sciences and Statistics, and is an Assistant Professor in the departments of Computer Sciences, Mathematics and Statistics in both, the College of Education and the College of Health Sciences in Abha, Saudi Arabia. A Voiceover, Audio Narrator and Dubbing Actor. [. . .]

Throwing up

I'm throwing up,
Yes, throwing up!
I curse the genes that bound me to the human race
And handed me over to this chaos

I wish I were a mangy or a Shirazi cat,
A mad or a well-bred dog.
I don't care,
I wish I were a little bird,
Or a fly teeming with microbes from dumpsites,
Endowed with a pair of wings
To go far away and pull my soul
Out of this stinking human neurotic pit

Oh . . .
I'm searching for an exit.
I'm suffocating and floating in nausea.
Thick foam is choking me and no way to stop that!

Translated by Norddine Zouitni

Elena Liliana Popescu (Romania) has a Ph.D. in Mathematics and is a professor at the University of Bucharest. She is a member of the Writers' Union of Romania and the Romanian PEN Centre. She has published 60 books of poetry and translations. Some of her poems have appeared in more than 100 literary magazines in 30 countries.

Pelerin

I

Nu sunt decât un gând al tău, înaripat
doar să călătoresc prin ere-mi este dat
prin lumi îndepărtate să trăiesc, să mor
și să-mi continuu zborul, de zeu rătăcitor . . .

De vise plutitoare ademenit să fiu
să cred în vraja fetei morgana din pustiu
să nu-mi aduc aminte menirea ce mi-ai dat
s-aleg mereu eroarea, să fiu neîmpăcat,

Să uit izvoru-mi sacru, din ce în ce mai mult
de-a inimii solie să nu știu să ascult
și să trăiesc coșmarul până la capăt: ura
și moartea deopotrivă să-mi fie semnătura,

Să port război zadarnic cu alte seminții
s-adun fără odihnă imense bogății
să-mi fie egoismul cuvânt de căpătâi
și dintre oameni lașul să-mi pară cel dintâi,

Credința proclamată să-mi fie vorbă-n vânt
deși o predic zilnic, să nu cred în cuvânt,
să mint cu ușurință și să răstălmăcesc
să vreau sub stăpânire tot neamul omenesc,

Să nu-nțeleg că viața e-un dar neprihănit
să risipesc aiurea talantul moștenit
să nu știu ce e mila, lovind fără cruțare
în cel căzut și pașnic, lipsit de apărare,

World Healing ~ World Peace 2020

Şi să repet întruna greşeala de-nceput
pe drumul amăgirii – întâiul pas făcut,
să ocolesc dreptatea în faptă şi-n cuvânt
să-nchei cu neştiinţa un straşnic legământ,

Nesăbuinţa, teama, să nu pot să-mi măsor
să nu ştiu ce-i ruşinea, să fiu slab, trădător
prin faptele-mi mărunte să preamăresc mereu
căderea în puterea făţarnicului eu . . .

II

Un gând al meu, într-adevăr, înaripat
în lumea de fantasme de tine exilat
şi rătăcind din loc în loc, neştiutor
să poţi cândva să te întorci triumfător,

De visele-amăgirii s-ajungi să te dezlegi
nimic să nu te-abată din calea ce-o alegi
treptat să redescoperi menirea ce ţi-am dat
să descifrezi misterul în tine încrustat,

Să îţi aduci aminte din ce în ce mai clar
de cel ce-a fost cu tine-n periplul solitar
să-i faci iubirii cale, în inimă s-o porţi
şi viaţa să le-o aperi la cei treziţi din morţi.

Să poţi vedea în toate pe cel ce le-a creat
să ştii că avuţia n-o are cel bogat,
că universul însuşi trăieşte prin iubire:
să-ţi poţi ierta vrăşmaşul e-nscris în a ta fire.

Credinţa ta va creşte din ce în ce mai mare
de când te vei supune la singura-ncercare,
să cauţi adevărul: a fi sau a nu fi?
Stăpân pe tine însuţi vei reuşi să fii!

World Healing ~ World Peace 2020

Vei şti atunci că viaţa e fără de sfârşit
şi-ntreaga moştenire ce crezi c-ai risipit
te-aşteaptă înmiită, al ei stăpân sortit,
când centrul minţii tale va fi nemărginit . . .

Vei căuta-nceputul şi nu-l vei mai găsi
în saltul cel din urmă pe care-l poţi gândi
spre ţara ta natală-n cel mai umil veşmânt
purificat şi liber de orice legământ.

Acolo unde răul nu are cum ajunge
doar armonia în toate, ce-s una, se răsfrânge.
Cuvântul, fapta, gândul în tine se rostesc,
întreaga libertate-n tăcere ţi-o vestesc.

World Healing ~ World Peace 2020

The Pilgrim

I

I am only one of your winged thoughts
it was given to me only to travel through the ages
to live in faraway worlds, to die
and to continue my wandering god flight . . .

To be tempted by floating dreams
to believe in the spell of the Fata Morgana in the desert
and not to remember the mission you've given me
to choose always the error, to be unappeased

To forget my sacred source, and more and more
not to know to listen of the heart's message
and to live the nightmare until the end: hatred
and death shall both be my signature,

To make useless war against other people
to gather restlessly huge fortunes
to have the selfishness as my main word
and between the people to consider the coward the first

The faith I proclaim to be but pure chatter
though I teach it every day, not to believe a word of it,
to easily lie and twist the meanings
to want to dominate the entire humanity,

Not to understand that life is an unstained gift
to scatter uselessly the inherited talent
not to know what pity is, striking without mercy
in the fallen and peaceful one, the defenseless one,

And to repeat ceaselessly the initial error
on the road of deceit – the first step taken,
to avoid justice in acts and in words
to make with the ignorance a tremendous oath,

World Healing ~ World Peace 2020

Not to be able to measure my senselessness, my fear,
not know what shame is, to be weak, traitor
to praise always by my petty acts
the falling in the power of the hypocrite ego . . .

II

One of my thoughts, indeed, with wings
Exiled by you in the world of phantasms
You are wandering unknowingly from place to place
If you only could come back, someday, triumphantly

If you could get loose from the dreams of deception
And remain steady on the way you choose
Step by step to discover the destiny I gave you
And decipher the mystery embedded in yourself

Also remember always clearer
The one who was with you in your solitary journey
Make room for love and hold it in your heart
And defend the life of those who resurrected from the death

I wish you could see in all things the one who created them
And know that the richness does not belong to the rich
That the universe itself exists through love:
To be able to forgive the enemy is written in your nature.

Your faith will grow always bigger
When you will accept the only trial
To find the truth: to be or not to be?
Then you will become your own master

You will know then that life is with no end
And that the whole inheritance you think you wasted
Is waiting for you thousand-fold, you its destined master
When the center of your mind will be infinite

World Healing ~ World Peace 2020

You will search for the beginning and will not find it anymore
In the last jump that you could think of
Towards your native country, in the most modest garment
Purified and free from any binding.

There where there is no way for evil to arrive
Only harmony in all things that are one surfaces
The words, deeds, thoughts are speaking themselves in you
They give you the news of what whole freedom is.

Translated by Theodor Damian

World Healing ~ World Peace 2020

[. . .] A postgraduate in Nepali Literature and Sociology, Krishna Prasai made his debut in writing in 1975 with the publication of his poems in the Jhapa-based periodical *Suryodaya*. Originally from Dhaijan, Jhapa and presently a resident of Anamnagar, Kathmandu, Mr. Prasai edited *Nepali Samasamayik Kavitahroo,* an anthology of contemporary Nepali poetry when he was just 24 years old, exhibiting a rare literary talent he possessed. [. . .]

World Healing ~ World Peace 2020

The Day I Wept

Ripples of joy had gripped the world!
While many enjoyed in freedom
The festive hours with fire-crackers
I was reclining, down with grief;
It was 29 May, 1953, Wednesday.

A man from New Zealand stepped upon my head.
Another man, who stood atop the hood
Was a porter from my own country
Who, in the long run, became a foreigner too.

The truth I know is single:
The Himalayas stand above us
And the nation above the Himalayas;
We exist because the Himalayas and the nation do.

The day Hilary placed his foot atop Sagarmatha^0,
And Tenzing atop his own cap,
Someone else rose above the nation.

That day
When Sagarmatha, the world's hood we revere as God
Shied away,
That day, when the crown of the world was vanquished
That day, when grandeur withered
Was the day I cried
Seeing my height diminish,

Getting a stranger's footstep upon myself,
Seeing you crown a man who downplayed my hood

World Healing ~ World Peace 2020

How can I call a person great,
Who crushed down my head
And is doing so, even now Krishna Prasai
Erecting a Pyramid of impurity?

I have a question for you, Motherland!
Which of your gods is appeased
With cash offerings placed in a temple
By someone who places his feet
Atop the idols enshrined therein?

I care not what you say;
I defy your old statute!
Say, where on earth the head can be crushed
After paying a fee for it?
Under whose rules can the crown be trampled
After some cash has been paid?
Which law allows anyone to mount atop the chest
Merely for some pelf paid thereof?

Presently, I am soaked with indignation and hatred
On seeing the rules your country sets.

World Healing ~ World Peace 2020

Née à Trois-Rivières (Canada) en 1951, elle déménage en Abitibi en 1971. Durant 35 ans, elle a travaillé pour la commission scolaire du Lac-Abitibi. Louise dit avoir apprécié ses expériences diversifiées, surtout celles auprès des enfants. Retraitée, hypersensible, elle écrit encore des poèmes depuis son adolescence.

World Healing ~ World Peace 2020

IL SAIGNE MON CŒUR

Mon cœur saigne à cause de toutes ces guerres.
On tue tant de gens et on détruit la terre.
On peut se permettre tout pour de l'argent.
Mon regard sur le monde est décourageant.

Trop d'enfants, notre relève de demain,
Souffrent et ne comprennent pas tous ces humains
Qui se battent autour d'eux en s'entretuant.
Regards tristes sur cet univers puant.

Péché que de penser positivement,
Espérant la paix définitivement?
Un de mes grands rêves depuis si longtemps :
Composer en poésie et en chantant!

Les enfants s'unissent et se donnent les mains,
Une prière, message aux citoyens,
De rechercher bonheur et sérénité
Pour avoir la vie et la prospérité.

Peu importe la couleur de votre peau,
Votre langue ou encore votre drapeau,
Vous méritez tous d'être bien respectés
De connaître une paix sans captivité.

Note: pour guérir, il faut dénoncer et bien diagnostiquer. Votons pour l'espoir.

My Heart Bleeds

My heart is bleeding because of all of these wars
We murder so many people and destroy the Earth
We allow these things to gain wealth
My view of the world is disheartening

Many children, our future
Suffer and do not understand this human nature
Of war and killing each other
Their sad faces observing this toxic world

Is it a sin to think more positively
Wishing for an everlasting peace
One of my biggest dreams:
Composing poetry and singing

Our children united and holding hands
Praying, reaching out to society
Searching for happiness and serenity
Having a life full of prosperity

Pay no importance to the color of our skin
Our language or the flag that represents our Country
We all deserve to be respected
To live a life of peace outside of captivity

Please note: In order to heal, we must denounce this injustice. Let's believe in hope.

Translated by Kayla Trottier

Naida Mujkić has a Ph.D. Her work has appeared in literary journals and anthologies around the world. So far, she has published five books of poetry and one book of lyrical prose. She has participated in several international poetry and literature festivals.

The Mother of an Asian Migrant

The grave of an Asian migrant
Is covered by tree shadows,
And fine snow
Nothing is sprouting from it,
But grass will grow, surely, grow
The grave of an Asian migrant follows
The history of search
Migrant 2018 Nomen Nescio.
He doesn't even have the present
But he had a mother
And she's now waiting and she's worried
Because no news is coming to her
She is lifting her head towards the skies
Clouds are racing above her
Full of bird wings flapping
She is holding the brim of a cloud
With her hands
And she would have stayed there, doubting
That destiny existed
Had the cloud not said: "Come back,
Mother. Your son is at the home of your heart now."
So, the mother returned, riding on the tears of ether.

Dr. Tarana Turan Rahimli is an Azerbaijani poet, writer, journalist, translator, and academic. She is an active member of the International Literary Agency in Turkey, Azerbaijan, the Philippines, Kazakhstan, İtaly, Oman, Belgium and USA. She has a Ph.D. in Philology, and works as an Associate Professor of Literature and Chair of the Azerbaijan State Pedagogical University. She has authored 9 books and over 400 articles. [. . .]

Good Morning, Rome!

Good morning, Rome!
Your sun is smiling at me
In the middle of the winter.
Let your morning
That is far from the malice of the world
Be full of light!
Land of Pompei
Where the swords
That cut the shadows of evil
Are shining from a far distance.
Let your mornings
Which are prohibited to oppression
Be full of light!
Hey, Fontana Truvi
Let your waters
That are purling
In the kingdom of wishes
In the intention of lovers
Be full of light!
Good morning, Rome!

Hey, tangerine trees,
On the way of Coliseum,
How good you grow here!
Your branches are heavy with fruits,
But nobody picks any of them
In the unjust fight
The crowns of our life
The tiny children,
Are picked up basket after basket.
Good morning, Rome!
Old, great Vatican!
Let around you always be happy life,
Let you always be flourishing
Let you never witness
To the blood that was shed in vain.

World Healing ~ World Peace 2020

Hey, the stage of theatre of Marcellus!
Let you always be lost in silence!
Be always so-
Being far from the "games"
Played at the world stage.
Enchant my spirit
Let be inspired and write
About your immortal fame.
Good morning, Rome!
I am sowing a handful of hope
On your soil in which poppies grow
In February.
Let those hopes germinate
And have a thousand branches.
Poetry didn't change us,
Let me dedicate a poem
To humanity.
Let me write a poem
To each green leaf of you
Maybe it might take wings
And guard over the humanity
Good morning, Rome!
Good morning, Rome!

Translated by Sevil Gülten

World Healing ~ World Peace 2020

Francisca Ricinski, writer & journalist, lives near Bonn. She is a member of the association of German authors and PEN, co-editor of the literature magazine „Dichtungsring", and senior editor of „Matrix". She has authored poetry, short prose, children's books, theatre plays, interviews, collages etc. « Car tu étais pluie » L'Harmattan (Paris 2019) is one of the numerous recognitions with which she has been awarded.

As If a Piece from Childhood Days . . .

I was wandering among wardrobes adorned with marquetery, waterbeds awoke in me sweet wishes from before and Florentine mirrors tried to hide the bores of a sleepless forehead. Yet when I touched the mouth of a carousel-horse, I knew that I was a child, who had many days behind and in some corner those many days were waiting for me.

Between the white-blue and clay-yellow houses I roamed; they were my colours. Red lacked, but I did not miss it. Too many flags on streets and markets. And blood-hoses drowning the lawn. Compulsive decor. But in the alleys, we passed through there was a smell of storks in love.

I ran between the cities with a thousand necks were defying the skies and scraping the birds' eyes. Through streets that had long lost their musicians.
Between numbers in lieu of people. Near the din, shoving the prayers to the edges of the world.

Preludes of apocalypse. I would convince the sparrows to turn homeward, to guide the dove back into the arms of Picasso's Child.
But how? How could I calm the pregnant women in their fear to give birth to future warriors or warn the virgins to flee from the paradise of Kamikaze-pilots?

Above all, the sky became the place where meteorites began to overthrow and people bought cemeteries.

I believed, a rotation is something that arises in body the life and let it die. But when I awoke, found traces thereof in the raindrops and their sounds.

As if a peace from childhood days would overwhelm me.

World Healing ~ World Peace 2020

Abdel-Wahed Souayah of Bembla, Tunisia is a writer and a professor of Arabic. He has many publications in local and international literary magazines. He has authored eight volumes of prose poetry, short stories and essays. His latest publications include *Two Summers Have Passed* and *Winter Is Not Here* (Irak, 2018). He has translated *Mémoire sous le vent* by Francisca Ricinski (Khayal Editions, 2019).

God Is Green

I replace my hands by two wings
plant other eyes in my head
get rid of ass completely and throw it to wolves
make my stomach in size of a rose
fill my heart with green
learn the language of birds and chants of wind
and fly up and search the universe for a new homeland
for another planet where I practice my life for the first time
see the picture clear in it
can undress
and get laid with sky at mid-day
a homeland where red colors and knives disappear
the blood-red is in my country, behind the curtains in the
eastern nights
in mosques in streets in space
in the brains and in the pages of yellow books
he blood-red hates colors and makes fun of dawn
I fly up above the Arab map
look for a god to paint it in green

Translated by Ali Abukhattab

World Healing ~ World Peace 2020

Ali Abukhattab is a poet, literary critic, translator, dramaturg, journalist. He has authored books and contributed to various anthologies. He also writes children's literature, political articles and cultural essays. He is the co-founder of the group "Utopia", which achieved many significant results in Palestine. Because of threats in his homeland, he lives in Norwegian exile.

Variations on the Genesis

In the beginning was the desire
Was going around the nowhere
Embracing the illusion
So, it died as smoke.
When it ecstasied by fact light
It got last in the silence of time.

In the beginning was the bomb
The god lighted its fuse
So, he dispersed as fragment.

In the beginning the apple was in
the hand of Eve
And Cain's hand carried the knife
Abel's neck bled
When Adam had eaten the apple.

In the beginning was the crime
It's the first and the last.
And was the spite
It's the visible
And the hidden

In the beginning the God wrote
his autobiography
On the kept sheet.
And when the destiny bewildered
us, we said, the peace is from God
and God wait at our door . . .

Parneet Jaggi (b.1975) has four collections of poems in English and two research books to her credit. Her poems have been published in several journals. Her name appears in the Directory of Writers in America's famous magazine *Poets and Writers*. Her poems are read and appreciated on world-famous sites like destinypoets.co.uk, poemhunter.com, atunispoetry.com, etc.

https://www.facebook.com/parneetjaggipoeticreflections/

An Aroma of Love

Love encompasses all piety,
not needed to showcase
in the splendour of colours and perfumes.
Love has its own colour – matchless.
An aroma,
that swirls inside the core of existence.
Hearts may be made of cells –
(living or dead)
or whatever else scientists may name,
Aroma touches the core,
spreads like smoke,
invisibly in the whole being,
emanates from the voices
and gaits of lovers.

Aroma of love embraces
all paths, isms and faiths.
A puff of locked gases
that can be locked no more,
erupts like a volcano,
flows down,
stratifies uneven lands.
Hot molten lava of love
holds the power
to eliminate filth of the world,
obliterate false fancies of ego-hatred,
erect love peaks on tall mountains,
hold the hand of humanity
and keep in peaceful embrace.

World Healing ~ World Peace 2020

Kimberly Burnham lived in tropical Colombia; in Belgium during the Vietnam War; in Japan, teaching English, and in the bustling international Toronto. Now, she is in Spokane, WA with her wife, Elizabeth. Her book, *Awakenings: Peace Dictionary, Language and the Mind, a Daily Brain Health Program* includes the word for peace in hundreds of languages.

https://www.nervewhisperer.solutions/

Sharing the Vulnerability Between War and Peace

Between war and peace is armor
in the Kobuk River dialect of Inupiat
an Alaskan language "aäuyautairrun" is peace
literally the absence of conflict
or spelled slightly differently "aŋuyautairrun"
researchers don't always agree
but rarely come to blows
over the best way to write sounds we hear
in the words of the unfamiliar

"Aŋuyałik" is war while "aŋuyaunnat" is armor
from the dictionary entries it is not clear
is the armor to protect us in times of war
act as a deterrent in times of peace
or must we leave behind our armor
opening ourselves vulnerable
as we move from war to peace

In the dictionary written over ten years of life
in Northwestern Alaska fight "aŋuyaktuk"
war "aŋuyałik" and soldiers or fighters "aŋuyiikti"
come before peace
the significance is not explained
leaving to our imaginations
why our instinct is to fight or flee
or send soldiers to negotiate a peace

What we must learn from war
in order to hold more tightly
to community to peace
to friendship to healing
and share all that we love

World Healing ~ World Peace 2020

perhaps we can understand from another Inupiat word
"tutkiksuk" is content, is solid, is peaceful
and discover a way to be vulnerable and solid
generous and content
finding peace without and within
ourselves

Pavol Janik has been President of the Slovak Writers' Society, Secretary General of the Slovak Writers' Society and Editor-in-Chief of the Slovak literary weekly, Literarny tyzdennik (2010–2013). His works have been translated into more than 20 languages and published in more than 30 countries.

Kosovo

A burning
paper Goethe
prays
in Serb
for four hundred dead children

In Schiller's stone eye
gleams a tear of mercury

There's a Gypsy weeping
for a little Romany fairy
at the bottom of the Adriatic

Blood
has an irresistible color
of the bluish dusk of the sky
from which falls
light and glitterings
like a gust of May rain
to fertilize the wounded earth.

Neetu Vaid Sharma is an award-winning poet and a published author. Neetu is a contemporary love poet. She is also an Assistant Professor of French and a web columnist. Her seven books include quotes and writings in two different genres – poetry and short-stories.

Independence 2019

After deliberate deep slumber
Yes, she opened her original mind-book
Crushed desires cropped up all over
A new life sunshine calling
Beautiful visions glancing at her
With graceful gait, she stepped out
To breathe freshly flowing fragrance
With fair hands she cornered
All the litter lazily loitering around
Space so serene spread everywhere
Mindfully she put on her iron confidence cloak
Tossing trucks of trash in world's giant gorge
She eyed her new self in the mirror
Heartily she murmured, "Delighted to date you!
Wish you real Independence!"

Monalisa Dash Dwibedy is a bilingual poet. Her literary work has been featured in many prestigious international anthologies and literally journals, including *The Year of the Poet* (Volume VI), "Galaktika Poetike ATUNIS", "Different Truths", and "Muse India ". Her poems have been translated into Nepalese and Guajarati.

Monalisa.dash@gmail.com

World Healing ~ World Peace 2020

Peace

I many times thought peace was near,
when peace was far away,
As a weary traveler deems to sight an oasis,
In the middle of a desert.
A lost voyager,
ponders how many fictitious shores
to go before finding a harbour.

Where was Peace
all the while,
Roaming in wilderness,
Or waiting for my homecoming,
In my high-rise condominium,
Handmade miniature kitchen garden,
At my so-called top-notch banking workplace.

As hopeless as I was,
I even thought of buying it
At Eaton Shopping Centre,
in a spicy slice of time
But Peace was sold out, invariably.

Until one day,
I found it within myself.
Sleeping like a baby.

Awakened,
Sleepy smiling eyes recognized me.
Ah! Finally, the moment had come;
I cuddled peace,
and never let it go.

Now we both are home,
everywhere.

World Healing ~ World Peace 2020

Ashok Bhargava is a poet, writer, community activist and a public speaker. He has published five books of poetry. His poems have been published in various literary magazines and anthologies. He is the founder of WIN – Writers International Network of Canada, a non-profit organization that nourishes and recognizes writers of diverse genres, artists and community leaders.

World Healing ~ World Peace 2020

Let It Be . . .

They will keep pouring in like sand grains
in an hourglass and slip through the fingers.

They will blow over like dust storm
if we build walls to stop them.

Ship loads of humanity will continue to cry
out loud before every sunrise on our shores.

Even if we don't want them to show up
and where else could they go.

Stop the Latino caravans and Haitian leaky boats
from seeing the glimmer of hope.

Syria, Iraq or Afghanistan: simply burn them to ashes
in the name of light.

Just a single ray of peace is plenty to fire hope
in the dark abyss of their desperation.

We can light peace
if we really want to.

We can heal the desperate
if we want to.

World Healing ~ World Peace 2020

Sandra Mooney-Ellerbeck is an internationally published poet. Her poetry reflects kinship with nature and world peace. She has contributed to the literary arts by being a creative writing instructor and an advocate through non-profit societies. Details about Sandra's haiku are at: www.thehaikufoundation.org. She lives with her husband and family in Alberta, Canada.

Yours and Mine

I'm suspicious of peace, yours and mine
when all works in harmony, when even
the household appliances hum as one.
When there are no new cracks
in the foundation, when the structure
of us does not shift from extreme
temperatures or all that rattles by.

I'm suspicious of peace
when the evening sky is the blue
of a Forget-Me-Not
signaling warm air arriving,
a cold front leaving.

I am suspicious of peace
when tulips rise, a constant hope
of spring, and when a day moves
around us like a cumulus cloud
offering reprieve from too much sun.

I've lived long enough to know the fragility
of tangibles, to know you can't even attach
to feelings. There is lack of permanency
even in thoughts, beliefs, suspicion,
and memories.

Sages say inner peace is all you can hold.
What if peace stretched beyond a smile
into a wingspan with a spirit of its own?

World Healing ~ World Peace 2020

Nassira Nezzar, a writer & poetess from Algeria, taught English at the university of Guelma and at the National Institute for Vocational Training. She has adored writing since a young age. Nassira has authored a book, entitled *Familiar Strangers*. She has contributed to numerous international anthologies.

www.wordsocean.wordpress.com

The Shades of Peace

I look at the horizon
Billions of stars were thrown on the dark
I look at the brilliance of moon
Many promises were thrown between later and soon
I look at you in the thronged silence,
In the rebellion of wars
In the thirst of peace
and the vibration of existence

Your whispers were there sitting
at the brink of dreams
In the mid of screens infested with
the sternest images
I take my breath while searching
the scent of the withering flowers,
while searching for peace
in the embrace of power

Oh life! A blazing sun
A glittering star
Bullets of death . . . Roses of hope
I feel the shade of peace should take off
the heaviness of dark and be bright
I feel the shade of peace shouldn't be aghast
To not let the internal turmoil run fast
Or be lost between the velocity of future
And the memories of the past

As always, as always
I don't search for nothingness
Or colors in the ashes
I rather search for your shining smiles
Fluttering away and reside in my heart

Clapping and clapping to the shades of peace
To your heart and to all what we miss
Listening to the whispers of evening

World Healing ~ World Peace 2020

Hugging the pure breeze of morning
Drawing the smiles on the soul and face
The shade of peace is a beautiful place.

World Healing ~ World Peace 2020

Anwar Ghani is an award-winning Iraqi poet, a Pushcart nominee and an author of more than ninety books. He was born in 1973 in Babylon. His name has appeared in more than fifty literary magazines and twenty anthologies in the USA, the UK and Asia. He has won many prizes, including the "World Best Poet in 2017 from WNWU". [. . .]

amazon.com/author/anwerghani

The Water of Peace

My dry life sits on that chair and looks at me with her cold smile. It sees my coat; it is not white because war had stolen our rainbow. I am not a gray man but my life is so pale and knows nothing about vivid perfumes. Yes, I am the war's son; my dreams are fading and my soul is a wooden tale. Do you see these fissures on my lips? They need some water. We didn't have colorful streets and our ship is too small to discover the sea's songs but everything will be velvety when our thirsty souls find some water of peace.

World Healing ~ World Peace 2020

The Tunisian poet Othmen Mahdi was born in 1972. He has published numerous books, which include the following: *Unemployed, The Will of the Rose, Demolition with Fingers, The Return of Poets, Color Memory, Pilgrimage to Washington,* and *Perforated Memory Hallucinations.*

https://www.facebook.com/mehdi.othman

The Recent Military Salute

Walk as a horse in honor of the service
Draw his memory filled with trolleys stuffed with unidentified bodies
Was not sad
But he did not rejoice when he gave up his weapon
and his military uniform,
his belief that he tied like an amulet to his neck
The recent military salute
And a collective photo with the fourth
Or the fifth regiment . . .
. . . not important
Shadow walking adjusting the collective photo in a frame
Not to mention that most of the soldiers would die in the fight
of darkness stuffed with belief
walking . . .
I watched him from the second floor
He walks before the fall
her
ch
u
t
In a narrow house it resembles a dirty parcel

The beer cans were without typographical errors

My fingers licked with sour anxiety

I kept wiping with my eyes confused by my losses

Hanging on a lime wall

. . . Yet you didn't come

Command daily, a little late

In a narrow house whose windows lean lazily on a field of wheat

World Healing ~ World Peace 2020

Do not allow a domestic fly to distribute its shit
On a faint lighting like a stolen kiss from an emotional bank
The fly stays out of the scene
 I kept setting traps for her satirical tons
. . . Yet you didn't come

In a narrow house like a shoe, it smells like a cockroach

I kept messing with the laughs of the accordion with a sweet boredom

And chew cannabis with a handful of pale laughter.
. . . Yet you didn't come

In a narrow house narrower than trying to survive a landmine

I breathe as a wake of an extinguished cigarette
In an empty beer bottle of green crystal

He lay on my back as a beetle

She's watching me from the books of Gaston Bachelard.

She is pushing her ass towards the "aesthetics of the place"
I was alone or I am the second

She saw me and reassured my day and walked away

. . . Yet you didn't come

World Healing ~ World Peace 2020

The poems of Sylwia K. Malinowska have been published in various journals, including "Poezja Dzisiaj" as well as in numerous anthologies in Polish, English and Bulgarian. She also writes poetry for the photo album by Beata Cierzniewska "Cognition", which was presented at The Cooper House Gallery in Dublin.

Natura

Beauty is a power flowing from the knowledge of our nature. The brightness of the heart, the light melting in the distance. Empathy and sensitivity in looking at other beings. It is a conscious value and intention that comes from the heart in action. This is following the voice of the heart when the whole world screams . . . no.

It is the forgiveness that gives solace and acceptance that brings peace.

Love, someone makes us great and the power that allows us to go on.

This certainty that pushes you in one direction although the common sense pulls you by the neck.

And although we do not know the future, we do not know what will happen next and we do not know why we are here, we know that it is our identity, the individual color that defines us in everyday life, separating the light line from the million others.

This power of striving for harmony and not perfection is beautiful.

World Healing ~ World Peace 2020

Dr. Sudarsan Sahu, a hydrogeologist by profession, works as a scientist in the Central Ground Water Board – a department under the Ministry of Jal Shakti, Government of India. He bears a poetic bent of mind from his childhood on. In addition to various other social subjects, he writes on issues related to the climate and ecology.

May You Be at Peace

When I stared at the sea
It's surging and splashing tides
And the birds that float and swing
The sea came in a blow
Of wet and cold breeze
That whispered in my ears and told
I'm at peace, may you be at peace

When passing through the woods
Listening the deep silence
And the singing solitude
The woods smiled
In a gust of wind and hissed
That whistled in my ears and told
I'm at peace, may you be at peace

When I looked up the sky
And gazed at the shining stars
In a night with silver dye
The night came closer
Through buzzing crickets like bees
And echoed in my ears and told
I'm at peace, may you be at peace

When I closed my eyes
And listened to the mighty spirit
Deep in the self that lies
A low sound unleashed with bliss
From far off in the hollows in mind
And resonated in my ears and told
I'm at peace, may you be at peace

Kamar Sultana Sheik is a poet, writing mostly on themes of spirituality, mysticism and nature. A self-styled life coach, Sultana calls herself a wordsmith. She has contributed to various anthologies and won several prizes in poetry contests.

sultana_sheik@yahoo.com.

The Butterfly Effect

Sitting unmoving
Unblinking, stony-faced,
Sulking, brooding, a mood as dark
As the approaching dusk;
The birds were going home,
All insects hidden in their crevices;
The moon was delaying her 'come-out',
The sun had set some time ago . . .
The dark mood getting darker . . .
Would it siphon me into sorrowful depths to sink?
Or would I rise to greet the stars, starry-eyed?
And then, you flapped your bright wings
With black spotted edges brushing my face . . .
My eye-lids blinked, lashes fluttered,
The movement in rhythm with yours . . .
Far away, the roll of thunder
Orange talons of lightning
Clawed the sky before me…
A WhatsApp message blinked:
A foretold storm had changed course . . .
'I', freed from the eye of the hurricane,
Went indoors for a warm drink
And a peaceful night.
You winged your way, away
To give relief elsewhere . . .
I promise to look out for you
In the next day's sunny morn',
You promise to breeze my way . . .
A storm changed course, my dear,
All because you flapped your wings!

Elizabeth Esguerra Castillo is an international poet and writer from The Philippines with multiple awards to her credit. She is a Global Peace Advocate and an Ambassador of Peace and Goodwill to The Philippines for the Naciones delas Letras based in Argentina. She has authored 2 books and contributed to nearly 100 international anthologies. [. . .]

https://www.facebook.com/lizzyecastillo

Peace Is Possible

We dream of a world enveloped in peace
Where people from all walks of life live
In dire harmony, love, and understanding,
A world where war does not even exist
A place of serenity, noble lives shared.

Peace is possible if we only take action
Let go of selfish ego and have the will to be selfless
Be like a child once more, full of hope and promises
And spread only love for all mankind
Wherever we may roam on earth.

The dove of peace with its immaculate white feathers
Can be seen hovering over the beauteous skies above
The promise of tomorrow, full of wonders and triumph
As we defeat all hindrances to attaining authentic peace
Peace which is longed for by hearts so pure
Awaiting of the dawning of a new frontier.

World Healing ~ World Peace 2020

Santosh Kumar Biswa is a Bhutanese author and poet. He is presently working as a teacher at the Damphu Central School in Bhutan. He is an inspirational World Peace agent; in which role he promotes peace in his country and around the world through literature. He is an award-winning writer who has achieved various recognitions from writers' circles globally. [. . .]

Just a Hug

Just a hug, then you're on the path of chastity,
The vanquisher of human's nous you become,
Not of the great power, but of the modest love.
Priceless it is, with values more than a life,
From the grave, that still can raise the death.

The warmth it imbues is eternal in its form,
At one time the fragile heart to resurrect again
And the stream of sadness to overcome shortly,
The smile, with the flag of new despairs to climb
Like the nightingale's song, so pure of passion.

Just a hug, chiliad grief surceases at once,
Hatred to be overruled, peace with a diadem,
Not through the narrow hole, merely the wider one,
For it takes no penny, but the credence heart
And the kinship to rule for the felicity to arrive.

World Healing ~ World Peace 2020

Penn State Emerita, hülya n. yılmaz is a published author, literary translator, and Co-Chair and Director of Editing Services at ICPI. Her poetry appeared in an excess of one hundred and ten anthologies of global endeavors. hülya finds it vital for everyone to understand a deeper sense of self, and writes creatively to attain a comprehensive awareness for and development of our humanity.

https://hulyanyilmaz.com/

the awakening

love and peace on my mind,
a cliché probably to many
though in-tune companions to me
both at once seem easiest to attain
unlike those of common artificiality

life keeps burning into Earth's core
gold-plated pen on imported paper . . .
insane politicians, disguised as humans
don their games of ultimate absurdity
against the wildest definition of sanity
each de-constructs, destroys and destructs
until their own brains shrink day by day
alongside ours, which we have evidently sent
onto lost grounds somewhere else to play

pain and suffering are all around
they keep dancing and prancing about
tapping non-stop at the heart of our soul
calling us to once again make ourselves whole

what will it take to wake us up?

take away the tears
take away the worries
they are Man-crafted, can you not see?

playgrounds were once meant for giggles
where have all the tummy-laughs gone?
what are we doing? what have we done?
broken promises, lost souls galore
tender hearts, unable to smile anymore

my friend, the wind sat down with me again
attempting to cleanse off of my essence the pain
there used to be a time when a gentle breeze

World Healing ~ World Peace 2020

felt aplenty to keep my aching mind at ease
the more i age the more i sink into a deep sorrow
for, hope is being rubbed from babies' 'morrow

what will it take to wake us up?

take away the tears
take away the worries
they are Man-crafted, can you not see?

i have had it with our caterings to vanity,
various types of insanity,
lecturing in wasted energy . . .
see me, see me, see me, see me!
look at what I have done of me, for me!
this is my personal journey!
why do you say it excludes the rest of humanity?

then, there are those
who say they speak for humanity
yet dress up in the darkest brand of nationality
including my own state of being torn . . .
what an extent to hypocrisy!

rapidly, we become historians
although we are the mere custodians
of our favored schools of thought

long ago, innocence was lost
no matter who now claims to have it
only a blurry line anon remains
atop the muddled bloody stains

in the name of humanitarianism?
what a glamorous facade!
why not call it what it is?
selective nationalism!

what will it take to wake us up?

World Healing ~ World Peace 2020

Teresa E. Gallion has published in numerous journals and anthologies. She has a chapbook, *Walking Sacred Ground*; a CD, "On the Wings of the Wind", and two books, *Contemplation in the High Desert* and *Chasing Light*. *Chasing Light* was a finalist for the New Mexico / Arizona Book Awards.

http://bit.ly/1aIVPNq

Ignited by Love

We can look at the universe
as a positive force or negative spark.
Only positive energy ignited with love
may lead to hearts open to peace.

To love or hate is a daily choice.
How may you find a bouquet of love?
I decide to take a long walk in the desert
seeking an answer to my pondering.

I walk for many days, cross many roads
and waterways. One day I wake up
in the Sahara Desert enchanted
by soft red sand, sink my feet into a warm

toast to a November afternoon and
the Sahara massages feet swollen with pain.
Touch of Nature tickles my toes.
Gratitude flows on the sand in soft shadows.

When I finally come to my senses, I realize
the most powerful dream to embrace me
gives a very simple message. Peace comes
when you surrender to the flame of love.

World Healing ~ World Peace 2020

Alicia Minjarez Ramírez is an internationally renowned Mexican poetess and author who has won numerous awards, including The Excellence Prize World Poetry Championship (Romania, 2019), the Literary Prize "Tra le Parole e L'infinito" (Italy 2019), and the EASAL Medal Award from the European Academy of Sciences and Letters (France, 2018).

World Healing ~ World Peace 2020

Healing the World

From the land of olive trees and argan oil
I raise my eyes to heaven,
My prayers flow
To the ends of the universe.
Every star as silent witness
Carries the perennial brightness
Of my thoughts:
Harmony, love, peace for all
On this blessed earth.

Let's build a bridge of words
To unite the peoples of the world,
Where goodness and peace
As branches of the wind
Shelter with poetry
Lost illusions
From other times;
Where there is no desire
To build more walls
Dividing our countries . . .
Our culture.

Let's tear down the walls!
Let's raise our voice!
To be heard only
The longing of our heart,
Healing wounds and scars
Of this lost world
In wealth and ambition.

Thousands of soldiers die
In senseless wars,
Without knowing why they annihilate
Their opponents.
Blood flows like an endless river,
Truncates the hope of parents

World Healing ~ World Peace 2020

Waiting to see their children grow up
In a better world.
We are all equal in the eyes of God!

Under this starry night,
I still believe that our actions and prayers
Can heal the world!
May our wishes travel through the cosmos and spread
As polyphonic aromas of myrrh, bergamot and cinnamon incenses.
Let´s pray to heal the wounds of our surrounding!
Let's fight to keep peace among all nations!
Am I asking too much?

Monsif Beroual was born in 1994 in Midelt, Morocco. He is an internationally renowned poet with multiple awards to his credit, and Morocco's Youth Ambassador of Inner Child Press International. His poems have been translated into various languages and published in more than 150 international anthologies, magazines and journals.

World Healing ~ World Peace 2020

X Planet: The History Room

Dear human beings,
I lost the words; I wish if I could spell a word
I am the blamed one, the only one!
And the coming generation will say the same
Our grandparents' faults.
I wish if I can tell more words
But I've lost all the words
Every day I see the moon, I stare to that sun
Above me that sky full of stars
Under my feet that lands
Breathing the same air
But we never value that homeland
Hoping and wishing for better world
Without wars,
Without hate.
Am I the only one?
I wonder with that pain killing my heart
But all my hopes were caged into history room
What could we say for them
But we are the blamed ones
We lost control and we let anger control our needs
We could not bring the change
We only brought the wars
Cause we couldn't understand
We couldn't forget
Cause we couldn't forgive
We just brought the history to the future,
To the present,
To hate each other
We couldn't learn
But we learned to keep hating each other
Without understanding each other
Without given chance to love each other
That is us, our beloved human beings' generation.

International Vice-President of the Jara Foundation Nepal, Eden Soriano Trinidad Blooms has authored a bilingual poetry book, *Eden Blooms*, which was translated and published by Dr. L Sr Prasad. She is currently working on "Symphony of Souls" and *Eden Blooms 2*. She has translated *The Casket of Vermillion* by L Sr Prasad and *Sun Shower* by Krishna Prasai into Filipino.

World Healing ~ World Peace 2020

World Healing, World Peace

How to attain when the wealthy and powerful
Finance the gruesome agitations and cause chaos,
killings and mad uproar on the streets of every nations
with self-vested interest for more power
to cling to eternal power and positions.
From Mt Pinatubo to Mt Everest to Mt Denali
The wailing like siren of chilling voices
could be heard chanting, "give mother earth peace"

The rich do not want any more to lessen their wealth
They always want to be on the top
Ruling mankind and the world.

"As the seeds grow from the depth of the earth"
This illusive Peace will grow too, I believe.
From the darkest core of men's being
It will unfurl the natural goodness of human being.

In every cry of supplications
Of the depressed and oppressed child-like heart citizens
who wish to live and breathe in a serene Universe
Even in the midst of a calamity prone island of the Philippines.
Peace and harmony parading
Waving for World healing.

Those capable of doing such atrocities
They do not read how we weave our pearls
How would they know our cause, our pleadings
For Peace to come in our innermost feelings

As the soft wind from the East blew giving off the sweetest scent
blossoms of our virgin white Sampaguita
A little kindness, a little love, a little concern
not instant,
but constant
chiseling like woodpeckers
creating a nest holes even in the stone
hard- hearted man.

World Healing ~ World Peace 2020

Young and old
Wishes and whispers in anxious supplications
Like organic oil and balms, we wish to soothe
Hatred, injustices, nation against nation wars

If we don't chant for Peace
If our mind won't be moved to call for Peace
If the innermost core of our hearts won't seek for harmony
The tones of our inner voices will make even our bone marrows
Our mineralized seashores and river sands
To cry out loud for World healing and World Peace.

World Healing ~ World Peace 2020

Zaldy Carreon De Leon, Jr., LPT, MTh, CEdD is a licensed professional teacher, researcher, published creative writer, and a theologian. He has degrees in Education, Social Studies, Theology, Religious Education, and other liberal arts from both secular (Bataan Peninsula State University and Gordon College Institute of Graduate Studies) and ecclesiastical institutions. [. . .]

World Healing ~ World Peace 2020

No to War!

A man should have lived a thousand of years
When defiance made blessing disappears,
They learned to obey not a word of wisdom,
And established their own offbeat kingdom!
Blood runs in the Eden, waters and soil,
There begins the history of their toil!
Once, a peaceful place to encourage life,
Now a wicked factory of swords and knife!
All battles begin in the heart and thought,
All wars start when pride and prejudice fought!
This song of battles will remind us all,
That war is the bitterest of them all!

Of ten thousand matters that concerns me,
Seven thousand were made of poetry,
Two thousand books to digest a whole night,
And one thousand for anything that might.
Of one thousand of these anything I see,
Seven hundred for God in hymnody,
And two hundred for nature and flowers too,
And one hundred more for others I knew.
Of these hundred things I knew with my heart,
Seventy were my lovers from the start,
Twenty for family, friends, or desire,
But not a single poem for battle or war!

With this ink, I'll write a great battle cry,
Unheard by modern men lest they die,
Save Herodotus, Save Homer and Sap,
But I'll use my Soul to capture the gap.
Modern men hear not what the ancients heard,
The same ears though, differently preferred,
While the ancients write, the moderns bestow
The gift of technology in their brow!
Listen very well, to these people I'll tell,
What is a war and how it should not dwell?
This, a hymn that I should treasure the most,
After it, I'll write nothing for its cause!

World Healing ~ World Peace 2020

War's a disease of pride and prejudice,
A plague that doze a man to flaunt off peace!
Some eyes may see him drenched in his own blood,
A rite between him and his ancient god!
A rat that burrows unto someone's mud,
A mud that kills the root of any sod,
A sod that whispers the clamoring age,
A year or two may encompass his rage!
In pride, it haughts the power in his arm,
Prolific mouth of disguises and charm!
A million knives that halved the world in two,
Another million swords to stab us through.

His arm's a rock of un-defining ton,
Too strong, too immortal, too much alone!
When it pushes the weak, the weak trembles,
When it tramples your wit, your life shambles.
In prejudice it holds a high posture,
You are belittled by his odd gesture,
He slaps on your face, he spits on your soul,
Never you'll recover from his scuffle.
War's a disease that's slow to heal, a grit
In the eye so harsh as to blind your sight!
A rage that surrenders a week of pain,
A boil that succumbs your innermost saint!

A thief whose hands were clutched indignant,
An old phantom whose face is full of rant,
Rage whose whip is to suffer his subject,
A blatant scoundrel who offends a sect!
Like a star from death pulls your soul to dry,
And so, as the light that made it thin and wry.
A burning forest, a fire spreading quick,
That man should have gone to waters and creek!
A hell that surrounds your uneven fear,
He who loses his incredible seer!
A trap that separates your bone and meat,
A dung baked that afternoon's scorching heat!

A hard rock that swollen your head when struck,
A burn that fried your bones inside! And skulk

World Healing ~ World Peace 2020

On your deepest horror before you die,
A glance toward the summer heat's good bye!
War's the beginning of all discomforts,
Neither pillow nor bed offers some worth,
But loam to shade your eyes from the summer,
Some flower-blooms that attends to your care.
A cloud that never bring up rain but drought,
Ruins the duty of the soil to man!
When not a single rain has passed his net,
Then many mouths will receive their slow death!

A comet whose tail is beyond our math!
The bleak clouds of fire atone his format!
An omen that refuses to tell the wrong,
A prophesy before midnight's ding-dong!
A snake whose bite will bring weary and gloom,
To dream, to rest in your eternal room,
A viper's venom, the strangest poison,
A black mirror that makes all illusion.
The claws of lion, a most lurid roar,
A monster's shadow hidden like a boar,
The pang of sorrow, the chase in the wood,
The gloomy darkness, weird songs, killing mood.

War is an emblem of all things negate,
Fruitless testimony of shame and fate,
The horror to come, the valor is not,
War is Charon, and hundred thousand cots.
In almost any place his game is best,
When most fertile a soil for gold and feast,
They take the gold and the women behold,
On another land, they're naked and sold,
Beauty is wrestled to fall on their knee,
Wrestlers were hanged and crossed without pity.
But still brave our fellows in their fight,
That four hundred years is no longer right!

The seas have given up her liberty,
To embrace the whole earth a mimicry,
Of years gone by, forgotten and dusting,

World Healing ~ World Peace 2020

Death simplifies the virtue of nothing!
Yet as stars fall like wormwood in our lands,
Is there anything more vivid or grand?
Than to see how curses of greed can bite,
Frost in the feet that catapults his might!
Weary hunters of the field losing hope,
To see another game, the storms did sham,
Fallen swift like dark waters in their eyes,
An owl howling for desperate mice.

In the East are common these monstrous arts,
To question war's like to question the Tsar!
The soil of giver was taken by greed,
Their bellyful of meat's as fat as their creed!
Then people will rise against his great see,
To drown his face to death without mercy,
In blood he rules, in blood he'll be taken,
His heart's a black stone, they kept as a token.
Then all these people will unite to sing,
This poem of mine, a battle hymn, so bring
The band of trumpets, of bugles and lyre,
And let's start to sing in his jolly pyre!

'A small world has faced once again a war,
The sounds of bombings are heard from afar!
Men were needed badly the hour I said,
My lovers are many, I need not a raid,
The church bells ringing, the birds were confused,
We just got our blessings, we can't refuse!
The shouts of cannons, the shrills of bullets,
The marching snare-boys and army completes.
But all these will end only if we stand
Against war and not against someone's land!
Against war and not against one's culture,
Then, we will be happy, our peace assured.'

P.S. Bring this song to someone you know,
Who wants but to face tomorrow,
And tell him thus, our peace is sure,
Not one child's lost, not one life's lure.

World Healing ~ World Peace 2020

Romeo R. Agustin, Jr. is a licensed teacher and researcher at Balanga Elementary School. He has a Bachelor's and a Master's degree, and is currently finishing his doctorate in Education at the Bataan Peninsula State University in the Province of Bataan, The Philippines.

World Healing ~ World Peace 2020

War and Peace

There is no gladness or joy in any way
When, without peace, the heart is torn.
No smile, yet pretensions overtake

A soul, while happiness is not yet born.
There, in the plane of happiness went
Every dreams and hopeful source,

Yet within the emptiness, darkness
Ruled the heart when peace subsides
In the pillows of the dying breath.

Angels are no longer, but death they were,
Emptiness roam about, tears in full,
Then silence pretends to be serene

When, in truth, there is no one left
To carry the burden of joy and a smile
When everyone is at their darkest days.

There is no gladness or joy in any way
When, in any chance forbids us peace,
the heart is torn, and ends up a failure.

Metin Cengiz (b. 1953 in Kars-Göle, Turkey), published sixteen books of poems – many of which have been translated into about thirty languages and published in thirteen countries, and twenty books of theory and criticism on poetry. He has translated and published the poetry of about twenty poets from different countries. He has received numerous awards in his country and abroad. [. . .]

At War

At first war entered into our life by words
As if it was coming to us from the countryside
Even birds were carrying bullets for soldiers.
We didn't know it came on godly feet
Jumping from city to city
Entering into the games poor children played.
Desperate people ate it with their bread
The government spread it like honey on our bread
While soldiers thundered on streets.
Lovers cut short making love
But I took shelter in love making day by day.
Then it entered our songs with its terror
As if strangling us when we breathed
It was far from our homes, but within us
For days we made it side dish by our *rakı*
It was like drinking without water, but it happened
And some of us became heroes when we drank too much
And ceased fire, for a moment, on the battlefront.
Bread was twenty times more expensive
Our lovers changed their men madly
Our parents died while waiting for peace
We became parents while waiting for peace
We couldn't understand why the war didn't end
Then we came to know that with our tiny war didn't end
Then we came to know with our tiny minds
That the tumor grows within us
And dear reader, this tumor is you.

Translated by Müesser Yeniay

Ibrahim Honjo is a Canadian author of 29 books in Serbo-Croatian and English. His literary work has appeared in more than 30 anthologies and numerous magazines and newspapers. Some of his poems were translated into Italian, Korean, Spanish, Mongolian, Slovenian, Polish, German and Bahasa (Malesia).

World Healing ~ World Peace 2020

Symbols and Dilemmas

What are you doing in this dark evening
While you are praying
While you are serving him
While you are lying to us
While you are accusing us
And while you are judging us

What you are doing in this wretched evening
While you are praying
While you are uttering
Kill
Hate
Destroy
Set on fire
Cut somebody's throat
Rape
Rob

What are you doing in this poor evening
While you pray
And utter all these destructive words
And glorify his name
Not fearing his judgment

I listen and see
And I don't know what that means
Where everything leads
I know the innocent will suffer
They will pay for who knows how many times
Because you need new billions
You need to build your new world
You build and the people pay, pay, pay
And building and paying never end
Because you need more, more and more

World Healing ~ World Peace 2020

I know all your wishes and all your vices
I know all your plans and dreams and prophets
I know all about your greed and curse
I know all about your ignorance
And I am asking myself each day
Oh God, what are they doing
With my heart in your name

The sphinx of life never answered
The words sank into the walls of silence

I pray in my knowledge and ignorance
Oh God, stop them
Show them the path of love
And tell them that there are no "their" people
There are only people
All people are equal before you
Please God tell them the truth
And show them your ways
Rescue them and free them of greed and madness

I prayed and I am still praying
Does anybody hear my prayer?
Stone silence is echoing in my ears
Emptiness is settling in my look and soul
The worry for human beings is coming back as an unhappy thought
While the sphinx of life in me is asking again
People, what you doing to people in this dark evening
While you are praying to him
Uttering all these destructive words
What you are doing in my heart
On this planet soaked with blood for centuries
What you are doing in my heart and in his name

World Healing ~ World Peace 2020

Shiv Raj Pradhan is a Gandhian social worker at the front belt of a life zone. He has composed poems for contests which were organized by various poetry organizations around the world. His poems have appeared in numerous anthologies globally.

The Peace Symphony

For the hatred, the resistance entry is embrace.
For the anger, the resistance entry is smile.
For the rudeness, the resistance entry is politeness.
For the violence, the resistances entry is peace.
For the injustice, the resistance entry justice.
For the oppression, the resistance entry is kindness.
For mockery, the resistance entry is tolerance
For the ferocity, the resistance entry is nonviolence.
For the defeat, the resistance entry is victory.
For sin track, the resistance entry is righteousness.
For the poison, the resistance entry is nectar.
For the ruthlessness, the resistance entry is love and peace.

Peace, by all means, is version base of life
Peace is feat of unimpaired pursuit dive.

World Healing ~ World Peace 2020

Hema Ravi is a freelance trainer for IELTS and Communicative English. Her poetic publications include Haiku, Tanka, free verse and metrical verses. Her writings in Hindu have been published in New Indian Express, Femina, Woman's Era, and several online and print journals. Several of her haiku and form poems have been prize winners. [. . .]

hemaravi24@gmail.com

The Proximity

Let us dance, be merry, let there be cheer
In the proximity let our hearts blend
Let the winds be favourable, not veer.
Past dreary sands, choppy seas as we wend

In the proximity let our hearts blend
Let us sow the seeds of tender, loving care
Past dreary sands, choppy seas as we wend
Not succumbing to delusion or snare

Let us sow the seeds of tender loving care
Nurture sprouts to their best potential
Not succumbing to delusion or snare
For our own peace it is essential

Nurture sprouts to their best potential
Past dreary sands, choppy seas as we wend
For our own peace it is essential
In the proximity, let our hearts blend.

World Healing ~ World Peace 2020

Nicholas Shifrar dropped a Ph.D. program to write poems. He likes poems. He is from Salt Lake City, and presently resides in State College, PA. He has a Master's degree in arts from the University of Chicago, but doesn't brag about that. He brags about his friends because he loves his friends.

@NicholasShifrar

World Healing ~ World Peace 2020

Love XII

My lover is a muse.
She is my music, my peace, my suffering's sweet release.
She is my harmony and rhythm, the crescendo, the pianissimo
Of the songs like morning's light arising from the port town of my youth.
She is the resolution of dissonance and the dissonance of living
She is living well with wine and jazz and songs for drinking
The smacks of beer steins held by merry fists upon the tables
To make it to the cozy home so late that candles and her eyes
Are the only glows inside. She is my music she is my peace.
She lays with me to rest and begins again my morning with her song.

My muse is the wind.
She is the cuddling warm breeze atop a mountain in Spring
Descended swiftly through the trees beside the sea.
She pushes my sails from harbors failed and to the venture
Against her tempest. I pray. I pray in fear of her dark whirl
That crushes ships and ends a man and can end all men
Who are just there to stay afloat and make it to another side.
She tempts as tempests do but seek I do her calmest touch
Through all the tallest walls of waves and Poseidon's deepest punch.
She is my wind of safety longing, fear and tremble dawning.
She is my wind and I do love her.

My muse is a word
A seabird beneath bluest skies that breath
Poem and poem again like longing when no relatives
Or friends have thoughts or plans or just a chat to chat
To keep the silence at bay. The sky is solid silence.
And yet this bird is solace gliding and saying
That hollow days are not in fact empty and the sky
Has a language if you attune to blues that sing
And to the frequency of this and her and her and that
And then no loneliness can take you, no quiet can sink you back
And here beneath the honey sun I hear her words
Her words she sends a'dripp'n down like trickling streams.
Tickled golden sounds I heark, I heark:

World Healing ~ World Peace 2020

    Love me do you do
    And I to you and you again
    And then a we and yes, a we
    So sweet and sweet the taste of tongue
    That taps a pallet ten times each take
    Then 2nds, 3rds the time you said my love
    I love you yes, I do my love I love my love
    And that is you.

So here beneath those bluest skies and scorching sun
Your poem your poem it has begun and I to see
How shapes around do shape to sounds like clouds
That say most anything. The thing is, the earth, she speaks
And all I need is her.

My muse is a text.
Bear with me here my dear my dear
To read aloud with company I need a breath
A moment long to cover shy my down-turned eyes
When days have stretched up out the waking skies
A book we'll pick I'll read to you till morning's light
And rock the ship all through the night with dreams
And Gods the Bible holds and yes, the Greeks and tales of old
In accents ancient far and near to stay we'll make a joy through day and days
Anew I'll read to you each sentence fresh a leaping fish
For hungry sights and child delights that creatures small
And large have play in oceans' depths and trails that blaze.
I'll command Pharaoh to set us free and he will hear
That stand I firm with hand held high each weary sigh my lover makes
Enflames me bright a thousand candles fiercely fight
For nothing but your bare back side by which my skin shall hold.
And my fiction is but true for love I do yes all of you through and through
And through both any and all things. Through both any and all things.

My muse is hope and faith and fate and love (yes love I say and
Say again) my muse you are them all my 'magination's ways.
I'll settle slow from all these tales my ship sets down and down my sails
Again, I'll journey through all these to find the hand that holds all things.

World Healing ~ World Peace 2020

While bricks stacked high hold tight the days of workers waging toil and fray
Anxieties building boss and bills the shrill of yelling honks and hells
The modern life screams us awake for peace is not a static state
It is the night of hard rest earned and wars fought for trouble turned
To gifts of music, words, and fun which why is I can never run
A fight, a warrior brazen man with chest puffed out and weaponed hand
For stronger be the man of peace and that is why I'll war to seek
The quiet of your known embrace that death itself could ne'er erase
One day my heav'n will be a kiss and this is bliss
The kind that time cannot contain it keeps me here again again
And to the never never end.

World Healing ~ World Peace 2020

Mamu Roshid is a budding Rohingya poet from Myanmar. He has been using his experience in teaching English since the time he taught at the Bangladesh Learning Center in a Refugee Camp for 2 years. Mamu loves writing poetry, short stories and quotes. Mamu's poems have been published in many international anthologies.

World Healing ~ World Peace 2020

Peace

Let's burn a fire in the beacon of peace
To highlight our path of great activity
In a jocular life with glamor
And displaying one-hundred-percent useful positivity

Let's burn a fire in the beacon of peace
To polish all the structures of humanity
To serve apathy of discrimination
To kill the dark soul of discrimination

Let's add a kerosene in the beacon of peace
Bring the nation to light with compatibility
And bring a bright illumination of futility
Combination of a bright animation and with munition

Let's add a kerosene in the beacon of peace
Explain harmony and affection
From great freedom as great security
This or all areas of that country.

Houda Elfchtali_is President of the Moroccan Art and Culture Association ERATO, a Maghred countries delegate for "Motivational strips" – an international poetry forum, a Meknes / Morocco delegate for "100 Thousand Poets for Change" and for "Afropoesie", and literary consultant for the Forum of Poetry in India. [. . .]

Heal Yourself

Touch your innocence
Assume its powers
Stick to its bliss
. . . Win

Trust your purity
Dive in it
And then emerge
. . . Heal

Listen to your inward talk
Analyze it
Poetize it
. . . Grow

Befriend yourself
Love yourself
. . . Live

Question the world
Doubt it
. . . Know

Wonder in life
Wander in it
Leave traces
. . . Be

Love the words
Let them love you
Give them sense
Make them dance
. . . Exist

World Healing ~ World Peace 2020

Embrace your being
Preserve it
Defend it
. . . Survive

Write your story
Tell its chapters
. . . Share

Contemplate the Universe
Feel its components
. . . Care

Defy the days
Be a doer
. . . Act

Read the masters
Listen to them
Be amazed
. . . Learn

Exhale blackness
Inhale the lights
. . . Bloom

Fly high
Kiss the stars
Shine like them
. . . Love

Brian Callahan is almost 60 years of age. He is currently retired because of a disability as a result of a heart attack and a stroke. He has read over 300 novels in his lifetime. Presently, he is trying to become a writer / poet.

Weblink: Uncle B-rock's World

World Healing ~ World Peace 2020

2050

It will probably take that long
To stamp out hate, corruption,
Exclusion, and injustice, that's
So rampant in this world's (dis)order.
Gender equality will sum up by then
Socialism won't be a dirty word
Economic mathematics will even out
Cipher of the poor will be no Moor

Climate change will be a thing of the past
As seasons become normal
And the weather more formal
A result of the hard work and
Determination of the young
Who sees what's going on
With the politics that downplayed
Global warming. The butterfly-effect
Next human technology at it's best.

Arm sales and armies will be to defend
Nations for that sole purpose;
Police and states will serve and protect
The community as it should . . . US
Their will be a peaceful resolution
In the Middle East and the United
Nations will ensure it's international
Stage is a political example-world unity

Public dissent as well as the press
Will be allowed to protest and inform.
Non-violence will be the norm, devoted
The young will learn from their elders
And have the energy to set forth
The agenda of world peace- promoted

World Healing ~ World Peace 2020

Individuals will look within self
Improve and challenge themselves
To be better, learn to cooperate with
And value of respect for others.
Divine understanding, harmony will exist,
Mankind finally become brothers
Spirituality will rule. Nature and human
Nature endures. Creativity it's duality
Destruction will work together like lovers

World Healing ~ World Peace 2020

Caroline 'Ceri Naz' Nazareno-Gabis is the World Poetry International Director to Philippines, a 'poet of peace and friendship' with multiple awards on that subject to her credit, and an educator. She is the recipient of several international awards, including the 7th Prize Winner in the 19th and 20th Italian Literary Festival, World Poetry Empowered Poet, and more.

https://apwriters.org/author/ceri_naz/

A Selfless Beginning

Been to the city
Where I lived a million wishes,
But somehow, my scattered self
Reflects suffocated silence;
Reminiscing the jamboree
I have joined in when I was ten,
Me and my childhood friends were waiting for falling stars,
Watching Venus and the Northern Star
Seemingly, twinkling giggles in the vast skies;
There was a sudden poke in my heart,
Can altitude fathom the seasons of my life
So I can start a legacy for the human race?
That must be a big goal, but with tiny leaps together
We can make a big difference.

I grappled for meaning, even answers to my lengthy questions
Quite a gloomy story: from muted falling leaves,
of the last tree uprooted
After the Ursula's attack, the Christmas tropical storm,
I morphed in tears. Self-healing.
I found that inner peace, while bathing in the rain;
My soul wants rebellion: Shout out loud to request my neurons
To be sensible and emphatic.

Interlude of different conquests,
Rhyme in a language called Resilience.
All of the days, even nights of a deep sleep,
I am scattered everywhere,
Yet, I picked up my selfless dreams
To rise and shine again.

World Healing ~ World Peace 2020

A poet, translator, and published author, Muhammad Azram hails from Pakistan. His literary books continue to be published widely and his poems reside in numerous international anthologies and magazines. His selected work has been translated into Spanish, French, Serbian, Italian, Arabic, Hungarian and many other languages, having been published in prestigious print and online magazines. [. . .]

World Healing ~ World Peace 2020

On Peace

I solicited life with few questions
To discern the decorum of peace
And reach to penetration
Of "Mania" that is known as 'Peace'
My questions flow like torrent
Like sand from a closed palm
One by one, one following next
And followed by the next
With a flowing hiatus
Tiny in temperament
But do have their free subsistence

"What is peace?
Peace is an endeavor?
Or peace is an affirmation?
Facet ties between peace and life?
How peace stream into you?
Peace is something that can be conquered with efforts?
Peace is a phenomenon that can be learned?
And what is peace that surrounds us?
What is difference between?
Peace within us and that surrounds us?"

After listening to all my quests
With concentration and consideration
Life smiled at my juvenile quests
And virtuousness of my subject
Then life streamed the 'peace'
In humble and courteous manner

O naive Man with innocent seek
You know what peace is and where it dwells?
It was there deep within you
When you were about to ask
About the orientation of peace
Expedition for and of peace from life

World Healing ~ World Peace 2020

But with every quest you faded peace
Proportional to the complexity of quest
From life and its living endeavors

What do you mean?
Requested in humble tone

Simple life is flow simple flow
Flow to a subliminal attraction
And it wants to flow and chase
That is incorporated within intend
It is it's crave command and flow
As Subliminal demands of spirit of life
But when anything disturbs its flow
Or something challenges the internal flow
Its flow gets disturbed and deviated
Clash and struggle with barriers and hurdles
Placed by wisdom, reason and justification
Make the spirit of life fierce and violent
It loses control on its own flow
And loses the control it communication
Within itself and to everything that surrounds

Ivan Gaćina (Zadar, Croatia) writes poetry (including haiku), short stories, aphorisms, and book reviews. He is the author of three poetry books, *Tebe traži moja rima* (KC Kalliopa, Našice, Croatia, 2014), *Tvorac misli / prolaznik u noći* (SVEN, Niš, Serbia, 2015) and *Okovani prokletstvom* (IK "Rrom produkcija" & Udruženje romskih književnika, Belgrade, Serbia, 2018). [. . .]

https://www.pesem.si/ivangacina

World Healing ~ World Peace 2020

Northern Africa Nations

There's no greater pain
than the one which a man inflicts on another
disrupting his generous hospitality
with "Trojan" in a hate cellophane.
A sword of fate destroys the tissue of life
with hellish forces fanning the destructive flames
while the forests swallow millions of heroes,
and colonizers dishonor our women
and enslave our children.
Why are you digging graves for us, our British brother,
while shedding rivers of blood in Africa?
Black days have wrapped our homes with a veil of sadness
while the desolate land is visited by temptation.
While we feed the pain with peace,
hunger with love, thirst with patience
the Shakespearean question "To be or not to be"
shelters the African continent.
We clear new roads alongside our ancestors' graves
hoping the rain will wash away the injustice
and a new day will bring freedom.
At least that is what our dreams allow us to do
and we owe so much to the future generations,
since no matter how hard we are oppressed,
we believe it's our duty to be better and more humane beings.

World Healing ~ World Peace 2020

Noreen Ann Snyder is a poet and the author of four poetry books, out of which three have been co-authored with her loving husband, Garry A. Snyder. She will always do what she can to keep her husband's name and memories alive.

https://garryandnoreensnyder.wix.com/poetry

World Healing ~ World Peace 2020

Peace

Where can we find peace?
Peace only through Jesus Christ.
Peace,
oh, what a beautiful word –
peaceful life,
peaceful home,
peaceful world,
peaceful earth –
Oh, what a joy that would be!
Will it ever happen?
No, some human beings
will never achieve peace
in their lives.
Oh, how sad!
Oh, let there be peace
on this earth, we pray.
Remember one day I believe
it will happen
when Jesus comes back
on earth,
we will have peace,
complete peace
over the entire universe.
Oh, what a joy that will be!

World Healing ~ World Peace 2020

Born in Algiers, Hamid Larbi is a journalist and a poet who currently lives in Montpellier. He is the author of various essays and poetry collections, which have been translated into Spanish, Italian, Russian, Ukrainian, Romanian, Italian, Turkish, Arabic, English and Serbian languages. His poetry mostly originates from the depth of the human soul that evolves into lyrical realism. [. . .]

www.hamid-larbi.net

The Humanities

Anxiety, agony and hope
Examining the idea within the inner self
An enlightened idea, an insignificant idea
That follows the mind

To be immersed so many times
To be amazed, to be furious
Travelling aimlessly through the Humanities
In the absence of light

It is there, face to face
A dialogue goes on in solitude
Observing it
And ending up stripped unveiled

Nasty appearances
Whisper of melodious ideas
And furtive tunes crossing the mind
An inner call to close the eyes
And sense
Where to
travel.

Ashu Arora believes that he is just a tabula rasa in the vast arena of poetry and wants to escape from the hustle and bustle of this mortal world by hiding himself in the vast maze of literature. He holds a Master's degree in Economics, and has published poems in numerous anthologies.

https://www.facebook.com/ashuzarora

World Healing ~ World Peace 2020

Do Gods Fight for Us?

It looks like we have seen more than enough
the way we make our lives tough
by constantly debriefing each other's faith
and trying to prove mine is best & yours, a waste.

But what if we flip this *onus probandi* the other way around,
and ask our respective Gods to pick sides on prig's battleground.
Would they agree to fight and bleed to death for us?
Or would they urge humans for their peaceful coexistence?

Some prophets might roll our tantrums into a football,
form a team and might play from dusk till dawn.
Some might leave us to our perishable fate,
And bribe the keeper to never let us through the heaven's gate.

But wherever they are, whenever they meet,
may be at a golf club or for the evening tea,
while offering *Namaz* or chanting *Hymns* at the Ganges,
I know they all pray for peace.

World Healing ~ World Peace 2020

Lily Swarn is a multilingual poet, published author and columnist from Chandigarh. Her awards include University Colours for Best Actress and Histrionics from Panjab University. A post-graduate in English, she writes with a poignant touch in English, Hindi, Punjabi and Urdu. Her poetry collection, *A Trellis of Ecstasy* was highly lauded on social media. [. . .]

World Healing ~ World Peace 2020

Burnt Rubais

Take me home tonight
Into the arms of peace
No gun shot sounds
No nuclear weapons
Only the frangipani
Perfuming the silver sky

Take me into the cavern
Where lions lie in repose
Playfully nudging their cubs
The lioness glows with pride
As the young one nuzzles her hide

Take me to that valley
Which Rumi talked about
Where all the songs
of Shams e Tabrizi
Come sashaying down from above

Take me to the lake
Where shikaara's dance a waltz
And shimmering ripples of waters
 swoon in the arms of Chinars

Take me inside the heart
That hears my burnt rubais
The ones I compose for him
Who would lay his life for me

World Healing ~ World Peace 2020

Photo Credit: Rromir Imami, Skopje, Macedonia, 2018

A 2017 Pulitzer Poetry Prize nominee and the recipient of numerous prestigious poetry awards, Fahredin Shehu was born in Rahovec, Kosova in 1972. He graduated from Prishtina University with a degree in Oriental Studies. [. . .] Presently, he operates as an independent scholar in the fields of World Spiritual Heritage and Sacral Esthetics. His literary work has been translated into a large number of languages. [. . .]

Aromatic Memories of the Past Age

The poppies even . . .
made it more beautiful
among the metallic sounds
of golden wheat leaves
on my most beloved July

Oh . . . that very age
I stood firm to expel
my inner daemons and
wrote the first verses
with the smell of earth
before it decomposed bows
twigs and leaves of ivy
sneaked on the trunk of oak trees.
A splendid petrichor!

Down there . . . the ravine beyond
my eyesight transported
                          all my fears
some demoiselle with metallic
                          greenish turquoise bodies
silently copulating to extend
                          their lives through
their progenies in another season
long plus millennia they shall live
                          in peace while we
the Humans grind souls
chop hearts and suck blood of each other

María Fernanda vila Migliaro was born in 1958 in Montevideo, Uruguay. She has a Bachelor's degree in International Relations. A writer, literature and Spanish teacher and a translator, Maria is a member of the Peace Council of Argentina. [. . .] Her work has been published in international anthologies. She is the recipient of numerous awards.

World Healing ~ World Peace 2020

A Poem for World Healing, World Peace

Stubborn rain falls on my head
Sun air climbs at my feet
Moon and snow in chiaroscuro
Sun shine dazzle peace
Make peace with each other
Let win many battles
Hate hate and love the enemy
Stop being one and be all
To be peace is to be you, is to be me, is to be a us
Peace without limits or horizons
Lark and Rainbow Peace
Peace in your hand and mine
Peace in the hammer and sickle
Be peace and make it, be peace and possess it
Be free and not be afraid
Peace at will
Peace in love to everything.
Sea and sky and sun and freedom
Moon and snow in chiaroscuro
Make peace with each other
Stop being ones and be all
Be free and not be afraid.

World Healing ~ World Peace 2020

Mounira Ahmed is Director of Public Relations and Media at the General Secretariat of Modern Literary Renaissance, Director of the Nafhat Al-Qalam newspaper site, [. . .] and Media director of the Palmyra Foundation for Women and Children. She has participated in many poetic and literary forums in the governorates of Damascus, Homs, Tartous, Hama and Lattakia.

World Healing ~ World Peace 2020

A Peace Toast

The earth condemns it and the answer is heaven
Soil failure awaits relief
From the window ocimum life
And a cup of coffee
His lines were drawn icon and prayer
She says come step . . . and with the rain we sow
For people for love
We sip cups of peace with them
O our motherland
Aromatic cleanse you with love
Embellishment with time reduction sheets
To glorify the universe with pride
Perfume
And dew beans spirit balsam
For wound sleep
Hey, Time Master
Come, come
Seriously walking upwards
For a little anxiety, come
These are moments from you
And leisurely sniping
Morning granules
From the cheek of a rose
Morning sweetheart
Time is calling out
It is the best time
Let the peace be the sewing thread and gather for it
Let's drink

World Healing ~ World Peace 2020

Azza Issa is from Egypt. She has a Bachelor's degree in Music Education, a diploma in Arabic music, and holds an honorary doctorate in Literature, Poetry and the Arts from Belgrade. In 2013, she was awarded by the Ministry of Education of Kuwait for her work in prose with the Medal of the Poet Teacher. [. . .]

World Healing ~ World Peace 2020

A Hymn for Peace

Pages appearing in the memory of days
Pain in the heart of life
Yellow carpets dried up
On the letters she was dancing
Within the range of dreams
Here the tables of the bereaved hearts
Here are orphans convoys
Here Spunts wail
In the details of boar
But she is still in her first innocence
Track the doves
Here is a character
The floor stands stolen larynx
Looking for an answer in the heart of Al-Jifa
Between gray visions and grave speeches
But she is still on her first tune
Seek the clouds
I did not know Taghired Al-Teer and Hadeel Al-Hamam
Cling to the roots
She sings song seasons
Wishes are grown by the land plaster
In the dark cavities
Love is the water of life
Times change
Love remains the goal of man
Blessed are the peacemakers
Blessed are the peacemakers

Mohamed Abdel Aziz Shmeis is from Cairo, Egypt. He is a writer and free poet with numerous awards to his credit. [. . .] He has founded the Al-Nahda School of Literature, is the Secretary General of the Literary School, and leads the Cultural Activity of the International Union for the Children of Egypt Abroad [. . .].

World Healing ~ World Peace 2020

If You Want Peace

If you want peace
You should proffer your hand and greeting
Walk over the sea
Children's dreams will repose
Above bridges of the days
Stand around them and cheering during the day
If the dark of the fate has come
On a glow of fire
Allah makes a reason
To wipe the tears of sadness
On a handful of dust
If you want peace, grant me your love
Return me my first days and renew all my dreams.
Spill your love inside my heart
And let me drink shores of the wine
Oh my friend, life is not an immortal tragedy
It is neither a gun for the fighter nor tears of the human
Life lives inside me without desertion or deprivation
And this is the question

Zainab Muhammad Aboud has graduated from Tishreen University in 2018 with a degree in Arabic Literature. She writes poetry and prose, and works as a language auditor in Modern Literary Renaissance, from where she received a certificate of honor. [. . .] Some of her poems have been published in Arabic magazines. [. . .]

World Healing ~ World Peace 2020

My Brother

With love we believe
In order for our peace to last
The religion of brotherhood
Our approach and medal
We seek to spread goodness in our forums
Those feats
We meant and spoke
Blessed are those with love
He honors himself
My brother
It gives you good harmony
We call love
To come true
The path of peace
Beginner and our conclusion

World Healing ~ World Peace 2020

Salah Zangana is a storywriter, poet, an essayist and a columnist at the Bachelor's Media Press. [. . .] In 2002, he won the Echo Award for Short Story in Dubai for his collection, *There Is a Dream, There Is a Fever*. He was awarded with the best storywriter-prize for 2013 by the Iraqi Eyes magazine. His work has appeared in numerous Iraqi and Arab newspapers and magazines.

World Healing ~ World Peace 2020

You Are My Country

In distant countries
Miss you
In exotic countries
I remember you
In the sad country
I cry you
In countries that do not seem to be a country
You are my country
I'm going to make a country
Of the remains of old countries
It fits our strangeness and our kindness
And does not age early
I will draw a warm country
Without walls and without espionage
I can borrow a country
Of history
Of tales
Of legends
We deserve
Worthy of this yearning
Who collects and hurts us
The country . . . all countries
It's you
And I am exile

World Healing ~ World Peace 2020

Habiba Gharib, Baby-boomers Oran, Algérie Titulaire d'un diplôme d'ingénieur d'État à l'Université Mohamed Boudiaf d'Oran en 1992, Journaliste et écrivain depuis 1993, Elle écrit en français et en arabe, Elle travaille comme journaliste dans la section culturelle du journal Al-Shaab Elle a été présidente et coordinatrice du forum des journaux pendant 3 ans Elle a une expérience radio [. . .].

World Healing ~ World Peace 2020

I Dream of the Human

I dream amidst chaos
Party, song, music and dance
From a haven of peace
From a trip to the land of humans . . .
I dream in the middle of a battlefield
Laughter and joy of a thousand flowers
Of poet and miles and a prose
I dream in the heart of the storm
From a bay with crystal clear and turquoise waters
Fine sand where the waves allow a break
I dream of the kindly human
Denying arms and conflict
Highly proclaiming his right to life
His loyalty to the land and to nature his loyalty

World Healing ~ World Peace 2020

Achwak Chaichi graduated from Al-Jilali University with a degree in the Law of International Economic Relations and has a diploma in architectural drawing. [. . .] She worked as a journalist for many Algerian newspapers. [. . .] She is Head of the State office of the Algerian Network for Cultural Information and the founder of The Little Literature Project. [. . .]

Lettres de paix

O noyé au temps de la réflexion et de l'analyse
écris sur le mur du souvenir
Les nom qui marchandé la paix dans prix
O venant du ciel
Distribuez vos stylos et fleurs de lotus
Les éleves aux pieds nus lavent leurs planches de bois sur Rafeel
Ils lisent le souvenir de la chance de rester sans épées
O venant de l'histoire de la guerre
La paix soit sur vous et la paix sur vous
Je m'adresse à l'être humain en toi
L'eau, le sol et le temps
Nous écrivons la civilization dans les lettres de grâce
Il m'a embrassé comme Eucalyptus a embrassé la sérénité
Demain le Phenix revient du voyage d'exil et de cendres
Nous enterrons les restes de trahison et de troubles
De mes mains, prends le rameau d'olivier et pimente les lettres
Le Temple du Soleil avec le Phenix Nous renouvelons
a esprits les salutation de la paix

Sumaya Al-Hamayda is a Jordanian poet who also writes short stories and socio-literary articles. She holds an Honorary Doctorate from the Institute of European Studies in Belgrade. [. . .] She is the Deputy Secretary General for Cultural Affairs in the Modern Arab Literary Renaissance. She has published *My Hair Demon* (in Nabati) and *On the Hill of Words: Pearls*.

World Healing ~ World Peace 2020

Resident: Peace

Behind the wall of Heaven
Tin bushes . . .
Embraces a swarm of bath
Water is sacred
Nostalgia . . .
Eats nectar longing
For ancestral land
And mud . . .
Seek beautiful forgiveness
In a suit of pardon
The most generous . . .
A vivid seek
Eat thorns of jellyfish
And heads of demons . . .
She shines shy
On the sun
Toward certainty . . .
Receiving beneficial seeds
A trail blossoms
The transients . . .
Grow on the banks of a river
Of Essen wine
Since the departure
The first two . . .
Green Branch of Peace
Passion
For the last three
Survivors.

World Healing ~ World Peace 2020

Abdel Fattah Shehata is a professor of Arabic, the founding member of the Renaissance Literary School and President of the Coptic Poets Association. [. . .] He has been a guest on all forums and cultural gatherings in Alexandria, Beheira, Kafr El-Sheikh and the governorates of Egypt. [. . .] In 2016, he received the Medal of Creative Excellence in Lebanon.

I Saw Love

I saw love in my country
Strange makes the picture
It relaxes our features
It wipes a squeezed tear
He sits in our wings
And erase all graveyard
May my country know it
It must be a turn
Learn from their little ones
Signs of love like football
She sings in our radio
Voluntarily unsafe
Wished for an almost approach
Of frenetic aches
Is not love in my country?
Mountains as its light?
Isn't it a laughing goal?
As games and buried
So we throw her page
And I denied the picture
We analyze what we support
And deprives others of his shura
We applaud if we approach us
And we deny him and his affairs
May God help him
He does his constitution
And it spreads our conditioner

World Healing ~ World Peace 2020

Emiliano Pintos was born on June 21, 1965 in Cunco, Araucania Chile with the name of Miguel Ángel Bahamondes Gutiérrez. For more than thirty years, he has been living in Argentina, from where he develops his literary activity. Emiliano has won numerous awards and recognitions from various countries.

World Healing ~ World Peace 2020

Freedom

As I return to watch that sunset
pregnant by dreams of tomorrow
hurry my promise song
That wants to vibrate with the dawn.

Don't talk to me about being a slave to silence
nor be the herald of nothingness,
I want to be the guerrilla whistle
that fecund, freedom with the word.

I don't want to be the scream in the desert
I want my voice to be heard
in the hidden confines of the times,
where the word is forbidden.

I want to be the pilgrim wind
that dries the tears of the soul
and the free will of Morpheus
Cut the chains that catch me.

I want to be Icarus, flying in belief
or a parable for years studied
I want to be who catches in your hands
The night that leads in the morning.

World Healing ~ World Peace 2020

In 2008, Angelica Cristina García has returned to her hometown, General San Martín, Peru where she has been working in projects of social inclusion and health improvement of the elderly. [. . .] In 2013, she started her own radio program. [. . .] After joining the commission of Visual Artists of GRAL, she participated in four annual exhibitions. [. . .]

World Healing ~ World Peace 2020

The Faces of Time

The face of time is atrocious,
Hurt like the heavy dust . . .
It covers everything . . .

His gestures densify,
They are not looking for any illustrious
It passes silently,
Like darkness and jealous hell.

Infinite and deep
Everything you can . . .
Nothing can . . .

Their beats lie together . . .
Linked, hungry for life,
Fed each other with the fear of not being.

They get frustrated again and again,
Mutating as life itself,
With the wild courage of today.

Time like the hurricane in its ravenous disappointment,
It goes through good and evil,
The fire and the cold summer
Covering the illusion aspect
With the pose of time...
Generous, affable, hermit . . .

Thus, the time so feared . . .
The dust so sure . . .
They could prevail in the troubled minute,
As sublime vestige of the trail of life.

Time takes from souls . . .
BUILDING THE GREATNESS OF BEING

World Healing ~ World Peace 2020

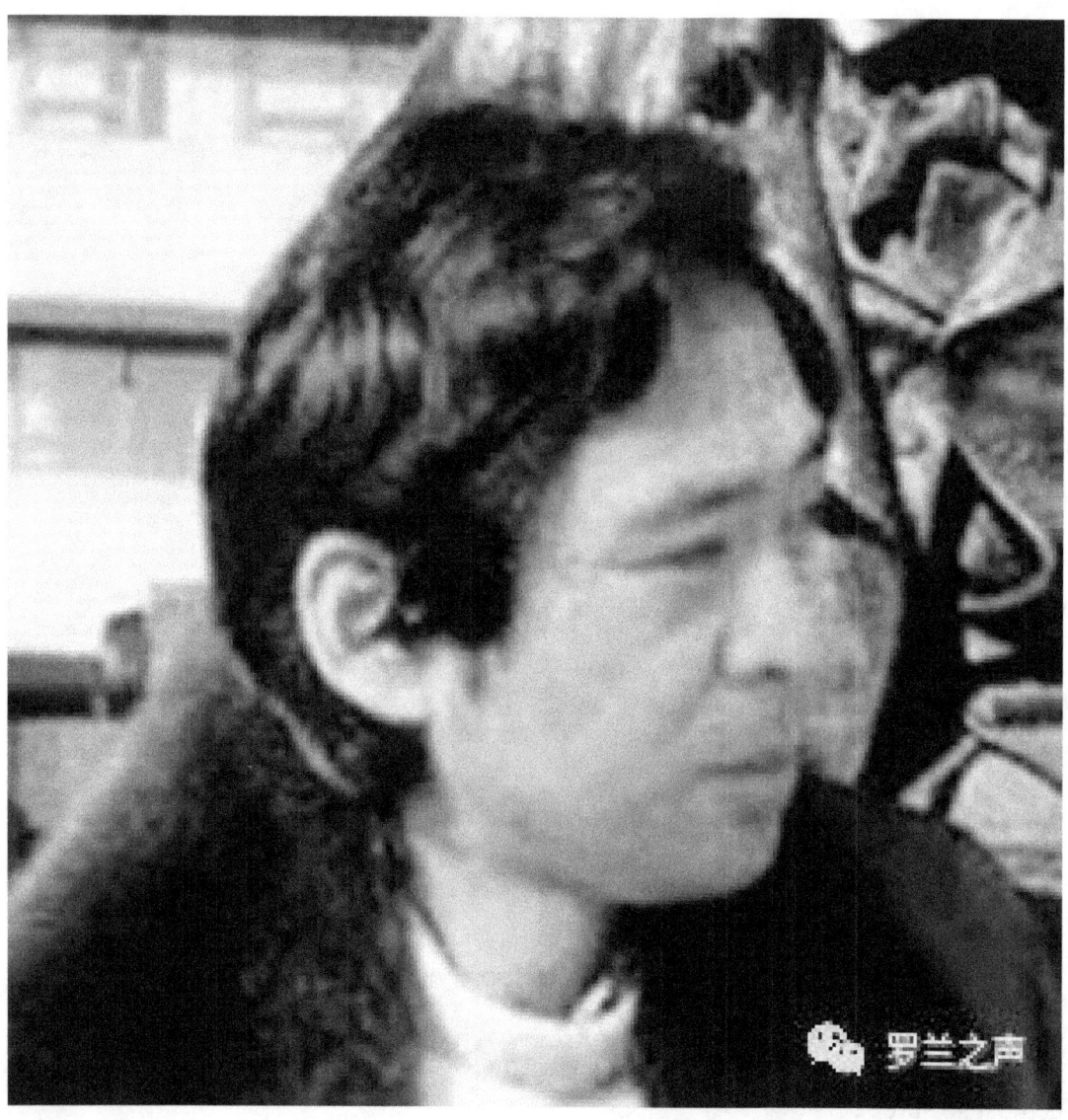

David Haotian Dai, a well-known bilingual poet, was born in China and now resides in the USA. He holds a B.A. degree in English language and literature. [. . .] He writes poems in English and in Chinese. His book, *The Cry of Wisdom*, is of philosophical content. [. . .]

A Peace of Mind Brings Peace to the World

A peace of mind
Like the serene blue sky
Covers the hurry and scurry world
A peace of mind
Like a patch of green grass
Holds birds and kids together

A peace of mind
Like a cup of cooling water
Puts out the fire of people's heart
A peace of mind
Like a white angel
Values wisdom rather than weapons

A peace of mind
Like a mercy dove
Weeps for the suffering of people from war

A peace of mind
Brings peace to the world

World Healing ~ World Peace 2020

Nataša Sardžoska b.1979, is a Macedonian poet, writer and polyglot translator. She holds a Ph.D. in Anthropology from Eberhard Karls University of Tübingen, Sorbonne Nouvelle in Paris and the University of Bergamo. She has five poetry books, *Blue Room*, *Skin*, *He Pulled Me with an Invisible String*, *Living Water* and *Coccyx*. [. . .]

The Swallower of Heights

First you must learn how to suffer then to love
otherwise you will spend your time on irreversible loss
confined transcription of reality
dust and desert
while pigeons are pecking
lost minerals of your bones
anything will be lost
however whenever:

You will be the loss.

Yet: does it matter
where you stand?

After all the blood poured for this cracked land
after all the wastelands conquered across the Levant
Africa and South America
all those battles weren't they enough
for us to inhabit one same skin and live together?
all those bloody shutters
screams stranded in electric wires neither:

Weren't they enough?

You will still pull out the distant times and dreams
in the abyss of your mind
in the crack of your body
blown veins and overheated suns
liquid fire and mute serpents
around your spine will be
cleaning all the dust in the world.

In this world
You are alone and alone you will be
alone you will win yourself
alone you will lose yourself
now you only have the duty to breath
to wheeze and howl and jump
as a child on an overheated sand:

World Healing ~ World Peace 2020

To survive.

Please
do not let them conquer
the valleys of your heart
do not let them get through
You are the only remained
unbowed warrior
the only:

swallower of heights

A 2018 Pulitzer Poetry Prize nominee and Inner Child Press International Cultural Ambassador to Iraq, Faleeha Hassan is a poet, teacher, editor, writer and playwright. Born in Najaf, Iraq in 1967, she now lives in the United States. Hassan has authored twenty-four books. She is the first woman to write poetry for children in Iraq. [. . .]

My Dangerous Memory

Oh, great!
Whenever I dream of birds,
the cages fly above my head
And I will need all my lifetime to know which cage belongs to my dream.
And then, whenever I try to remember my childhood,
a bomb falls from my memory and crashes into my reality.

. . .

"What a lovely sunny morning,"
I told the girl.
She was jogging in the forest,
and said, smiling at me:
"A soldier's helmet is falling from your memory again."
"Don't worry. I have so many of them," I told her.
Everything will be good,
I say to myself,
And I keep jogging from exile to exile,
as my friends keep running from the battlefield
of one war to another,
returning as pictures with black frames.

World Healing ~ World Peace 2020

William S. Peters, Sr., aka 'Just Bill', is an award-winning global activist for humanity. His poetry and prowess have been acknowledged and translated globally. He is the Chair Person of Inner Child Enterprises, Inner Child Press International and the World Healing, World Peace Foundation. He utilizes these vehicles along with his poetry and other writings to champion the cause of consciousness, peace, love, acceptance and compassion. His personal perspective is that 'life is a garden', and we must plant seeds of good intent, light and love that we all may harvest a sweet bountiful fruit. The 'by-line' Mr. Peters has coined for Inner Child Press is 'building bridges of cultural understanding'. Achieving this vital connection is his inspiration.

World Healing ~ World Peace 2020

A Piece of Peace

But a small slice,
But a crumb
That I can savor
That lasts me
For but a while

I am the earth,
I am the sky,
I am the forest, the wood,
The valley, the mountain,
The rivers, streams, brooks, and seas
I am the wind,
I am the breath of life . . .

I, we, see everything

I am all the creatures
Upon this planet,
That crawl leap, swim, float, slither and fly and climb
Beguiled by men
Sublimely so

Disease and Famine,
The makings of War,
With bombs and bullets
Shredding and shrouding
The atmosphere

Can we not coexist?
Is there not enough
For everyone?

Which, whose sons,
Whose daughters
Will push the button next?

World Healing ~ World Peace 2020

Whose sons,
Whose daughters
Will suffer the consequences
For which there is no defense?

I ask you not for much,
Do I?

But just a piece of peace,
And let us all heal together!

World Healing ~ World Peace 2020

World Healing, World Peace Foundation
human beings for humanity

worldhealingworldpeacefoundation.org

Become a member of the foundation

www.worldhealingworldpeacefoundation.org

Previous Issues

of

World Healing

World Peace

Available at:

www.innerchildpress.com/world-healing-world-peace-poetry

www.worldhealingworldpeacepoetry.com

www.worldhealingworldpeacefoundation.org

World Healing ~ World Peace 2020

World Healing ~ World Peace 2020

WORLD HEALING WORLD PEACE 2018

INNER CHILD PRESS

A Poetry Anthology for Humanity

Inner Child Press International

Inner Child Press International is a publishing company founded and operated by writers. Our personal publishing experiences provides us an intimate understanding of the sometimes-daunting challenges writers, new and seasoned, may face in the business of publishing and marketing their creative "Written Work".

For more Information:

Inner Child Press International

www.innerchildpress.com
intouch@innerchildpress.com

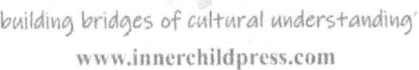
'building bridges of cultural understanding'
www.innerchildpress.com

www.ingramcontent.com/pod-product-compliance
Lightning Source LLC
Chambersburg PA
CBHW082108230426
43671CB00015B/2635